Ten Year Career

Ten Year Career

Reimagine business, design your life,
fast track your freedom

Jodie Cook

JOHN
MURRAY
LEARNING

First published in Great Britain by John Murray Learning in 2022
An imprint of John Murray Press
A division of Hodder & Stoughton Ltd,
An Hachette UK company

1

A CIP catalogue record for this title is available from the British Library

Trade Paperback ISBN 978 1 399 80320 5
eBook ISBN 978 1 399 80322 9

Typeset by KnowledgeWorks Global Ltd.

Printed and bound in Great Britain by Clays Ltd, Elcograf S.p.A.

John Murray Press policy is to use papers that are natural, renewable and recyclable products
and made from wood grown in sustainable forests. The logging and manufacturing processes
are expected to conform to the environmental regulations of the country of origin.

John Murray Press
Carmelite House
50 Victoria Embankment
London EC4Y 0DZ

www.johnmurraypress.co.uk

This book is dedicated to your success and happiness.

Contents

Foreword

We would all benefit from emulating Jodie Cook. She's an unstoppable force. Jodie introduced herself to me in 2016 after reading my first book, *Anything You Want*, saying she liked how, after I sold my company for $22 million USD, I kept my focus on giving and living instead of material possessions. Since then, she's impressed me more and more.

Her competitive powerlifting is further proof, through actions not words, that she puts in the work and powers through. That's extra-noteworthy in the field of entrepreneurship where anyone can call themselves an entrepreneur and talk up a dream. Jodie does the work.

When she told me she was writing *Ten Year Career*, I was eager to read it, but it's even better than I expected. Her overview — execute → systemize → scrutinize → exit — is spot on and matches my experience, both personally and of the other entrepreneurs I've known. It's the best framework for helping to identify where you are, and what's coming next. It reminds you of your endgame.

Jodie writes with generosity, always keeping the focus on you. She just completed a 'ten year career' path herself and has nothing to prove. This book is incredibly encouraging and helpful at every step, reminding you that you have the power and ability to make your ideal business and live your dream life. Every future millionaire needs this wise perspective. I highly recommend it to any entrepreneur.

Derek Sivers
entrepreneur, author

Introduction

I'd hardly told anyone I was selling my social media agency, JC Social Media. My team was sworn to secrecy, and only my husband knew the details. Throughout the process I made myself focus on the present, having patience rather than wishing time to hurry or thinking about life after completion. I made sure I didn't skip ahead too far, telling myself every day that it could still fall through.

Then the phone rang.

'Congratulations, Jodie, that's all gone through.' The deal was complete. The contracts had exchanged, the shares and funds transferred.

I was 32 years old and would never need to work again.

I felt an overwhelming sense of calm. Rather than rushing into making plans now that the deal was done, I looked back over my journey and where it had brought me. It had taken me less than ten years from the day I started my agency to completing the sale.

The average age of retirement in the UK is 64. In the USA it's 67. I was 32. My life had changed over 30 years ahead of schedule. But I'm no superhero.

Wherever you are right now, within ten years you could not need to work.

It's possible by starting, scaling and selling a profitable business for a sum of money that covers your living costs for the rest of your life. That's basic maths. It's also possible for you to feel retired, even if you never have an exit and keep working for years. But while it sounds simple, if you've started a business, you'll know that it's not. In fact, setting up is the easy part.

When you start a business it's great: designing your brand, creating your products or defining your service; planning how you'll approach customers and securing those first few projects. Fun, focus and learning new things every day. You love telling people about your venture, and every new connection or sale you make is exciting. The honeymoon period could last several months, maybe even a few years.

After a while, you might feel as if you're stuck in a rut. A dip. Perhaps you're juggling looking after customers with business development, as well as every admin task. You're busy, but not confident enough to delegate or relinquish control. You're not sure how to spend your time. Feelings of doubt creep in and you start to check out other options. Distractions tempt you.

You're working hard but feel as though you're not getting anywhere, clambering around on the side of a mountain with no track in sight. You're solving the same problems you solved at the beginning. You're not sure where to take your business and you have conflicting priorities. Your focus is waning. Perhaps you feel trapped. The future is unclear, and you might be having second thoughts about your path.

Whether or not business is going well, you still have questions in the back of your mind. What's next? What do I want?

Humans act out of desperation or inspiration to move away from pain and towards pleasure. In between both is a comfy middle ground where the pros outweigh the cons and things are just fine. There's not enough pressure to move either way. Many business owners remain caught in this place and never push on.

It's easy to coast but doing so might be costing your potential. Comfort can trap you. Hanging out there, you might start to think you're destined for life in the slow lane. You might accept that this is the way it is. You might wind back, take it easy and start to play golf in the afternoons. Most people, upon hitting this point, plod on, hoping something will be different. Others give up. They get a job, they try something else, or they settle.

There is another way. The Ten Year Career.

Imagine your life and career split into ten-year chunks, each one defined by something different. Each stage or chapter brings new discoveries, people and places, a new routine, new challenges. You rack up achievements and milestones, and make things happen that you never dreamed you could. You can bring a different version of yourself to each phase. Each one can be a new life.

Your career doesn't have to take up multiple decades. You don't have to finish your education, find a job and stick with it, progressing up a ladder until you retire. Your working career can be just one of many phases. In one phase you might manage people, another robots, and another your calendar as you travel the world. You could be an artist, a scientist, then an athlete.

You don't have to follow the same path for your whole life.

Not long before I sat down to write this book, I had been stuck. But after making and implementing a plan I was freed. I created a 'Goldilocks state' of running my business: not so much pressure that I freaked out and not so little that I lost interest; not so much to do that it monopolized my time, not so little that I lost control. I owned a business that I was into enough to care deeply about our clients, but not so deep that I lost my freedom. My team was self-sufficient enough to not need constant help, but dependable enough to thrive under strong leadership. I had a daily routine that was interesting and varied but never frantic. I was happy to stay but ready to go.

You can create a plan like this for yourself. Or you can carry on to a successful exit. Either way, your Ten Year Career plan has worked.

Even if you start today, at the bottom of the metaphorical mountain, you can retire in ten years. You could reach your ultimate goal within those ten years and make waves along the way. Wherever you are right now, how you spend the next ten years can define whether or not you need to work again. You can give yourself insane freedom and open a world of possibilities for what you do next.

It's never been more attainable to reach financial freedom and your version of retirement – which for many people simply means working because they want to, not because they have to – earlier than former generations. This will require careful planning, inventive thinking and an assessment of what's important. You'll have to dream big, create the plans and make incredible things happen.

I'll walk you through the methods of creating the Ten Year Career so you can apply each one to your journey. I'll show you why ten years is the perfect time frame in which to operate: long enough to always make the right decision, short enough to move fast and not waste time.

In the following chapters I cover:

- Mastering your mind
- Setting up for success
- Creating habits that serve you
- Living your version of success

- Frameworks to gain perspective and focus
- How to make difficult decisions
- Ways to protect your boundaries
- A method to design and lead a life you love
- A framework for mapping the phases of your Ten Year Career.

If left to themselves, your default habits likely will not be conducive to winning big and being set for life. The book will rewire and refresh how you frame your work and life for unimaginable benefits. Success will depend on your willingness to think about what you want, take the reins and do the work to get there. It's about steering your own ship, rather than seeing where the wind blows you. You're reading this because you want to grab the wheel.

For our purposes I assume you have an idea of what you would need in the bank or investments to no longer have to work. I assume you can roughly define your dream future, but you aren't sure how to make it happen.

This book isn't a quick fix for selling your business and retiring. It's a framework by which to set yourself up strong and build an enterprise with an endgame in mind. Nor is it about working out the specific details of what early retirement involves – it doesn't, for example, go deep into calculations, investing or compound interest.

This is not a book about making passive income. While I'm on board with creating assets that mean revenue flows automatically, I'm not on board with the pursuit of income for the sake of it. I don't think a business needs to be reduced to just its financial aspect. Solely seeking passive income is shallow. It's not endearing. It misses out the best parts of running and growing a business: the amazing work you get to do, the inspiring people you get to work with, the opportunities you get to seize. As it happens, focusing on service and significance will create passive income much faster than focusing on money.

This book won't give you a business idea or a step-by-step recipe on setting up a business. Trodden paths are rarely those that yield the best results. You can't copy and paste someone else's route to success. If you want what no one else has, do what no one else will do.

This book is a guide

Ten Year Career will be the trusted guide for you, the traveller. Within the chapters are stories, examples and questions to apply to your situation, along with a practical framework for you to use. You should start to see results of the methods straight away and realize how doable the Ten Year Career is for you. My goal is to provide a new way of thinking, open your mind, and spark ideas and thoughts.

Thirteen years ago, the seed was planted for me. I was 19 and working at my summer job in the sales office of Greenfield Print and Promotion, a small print and promotion company. My boss, Simon Greenfield, asked me what I wanted to do when I left university.

When I said I wasn't sure, he chuckled and said, 'Don't worry if you don't know yet. I'm 42, and I still don't know what I want to do. You have plenty of time to decide, and you have a good 40 years of working ahead of you yet.'

I stared at Simon. Forty years? It made no sense. What could I do in 40 years that I couldn't do in 20? Or ten? I had a feeling my career could be different than the one Simon had in mind.

When I started my social media agency in the summer of 2011, I was 22 and ready to test a theory. I theorized that I could apply multiples to everything I did. I could work three times as hard to reach a goal three times as fast. I could establish myself sooner, make a bigger impression, think harder, learn more and make better decisions. I didn't want to work every second of every day; I wanted to live an extraordinary life. I thought that by ramping up the right aspects and not getting involved in others, I could be free of the need to earn money by my early thirties.

For a decade I played a game with the goal of seeing what could be possible in ten years. I loved every second of it. During those ten years I grew my social media agency to be an established and profitable company, then oversaw its acquisition by another firm. I worked with interesting people and learned a lot about entrepreneurship. I travelled to and worked from amazing cities all over the world. I competed for Great Britain in the powerlifting world championships. I became a contributor for Forbes on the topic of entrepreneurs. I won awards. I made investments. I wrote and published books about entrepreneurship and entrepreneurial role models. I met inspiring people, including the authors of the books I read and applied to my game.

My journey started with a laptop and an idea. The ten years that came after progressed through a series of distinct phases, each with its own strategies and actions. Throughout this book I will explain how you can start to think in this way, to untold benefits. Maybe you already do, in which case we'll ramp up your intention to a whole new level. Many aspects of my process are replicable. This book is here to show you what's possible, and I'm here to guide you through.

'But how?' I hear you say. 'This sounds like a lot of work. It sounds like changing stuff. It sounds like unpacking things that work fine and making them different. It sounds like you will ask tough questions that I'll need to dig deep to find answers to. I'm busy. Do I have the time for this?'

You may say you don't have time to do this. I say you don't have time *not* to. The Greek Stoic philosopher Epictetus asked, 'How much longer are you going to wait before you demand the best for yourself?'

Let's begin.

Ten Year Career bonus companion course

To help guide you through your Ten Year Career, I have created a free companion course that includes bonus video content, worksheets, step-by-step guides, and all the resources and links mentioned in this book plus many more.

The companion course helps you apply the concepts in the book to your business to ensure its success, and I recommend you sign up right now.

The course is organized according to the chapters of *Ten Year Career*, so it's super simple to follow alongside the book so that you can get more from every chapter. Just like the book, the companion course is dedicated to your success and happiness.

I look forward to seeing you there!

Visit jodiecook.com/TYC for free access to your *Ten Year Career* bonus materials.

1

The Lies We Live

• • •

'OK, see you soon!' my mum said with a wave.

I sat on the bed and looked around the box of a room that was now my home. The walls were bare, the bed tiny, and the curtains a strange shade of green. I had a feeling that I was, too.

When my mum dropped me off at university, I was completely unprepared. I turned up with a suitcase of summer clothes, a chunky pink laptop and a box of cereal bars. My flatmates had at least thought to bring plates, pots and pans. My contribution to the kitchen was a spatula I won at freshers' fair.

Behind my confident smile and positive demeanour, I felt lost. I wasn't sure how or why I had ended up here. I didn't know what to expect. I didn't know who I was or what I wanted.

On the surface I was independent. I had worked in a restaurant since turning 16. I learned how to drive and bought myself a car with my wages the moment I could. But when confronted with three years of studying and doing exams, putting life on hold for a certificate, I wasn't completely sure I'd chosen this path.

My university degree in business management was another step on the education conveyor belt. I had played along for 14 years and somehow ended up in Sheffield with a distinct lack of cutlery, literally and metaphorically. Something was awry. I was going to figure it out.

Have you ever looked back at an old picture and cringed at your hairstyle? You might cringe because you never liked it back then; you were wearing it that way because you felt you should. Like many of my peers, I bumbled my way to this point without ever questioning whether I actually wanted what I was doing. With more self-awareness, I would have realized that I did not know how to think for myself, and that this would be a problem.

This chapter delves into the ways we are trained out of thinking for ourselves. Most of us live by outdated beliefs we blindly follow without questioning. Where might this lead? What is the root cause? What's the difference between thinking for yourself and ambling along? In these pages I'll show you the ways in which you can and should be thinking differently. Let's stop these unhelpful influences and limiting beliefs killing your gains once and for all.

Outdated beliefs

Sophie loves baking cakes. After carefully weighing the ingredients, mixing the batter and baking, she takes her cake out to inspect her work. She removes it from its square cake tin and proceeds to cut off each of the four corners, leaving it to cool before icing.

Once, when visiting during this process, a friend of Sophie's asked her why she cut off the corners. Sophie replied she did it because her mother always had. She called her mother to ask why she cut the corners off the cake. Her mother said she did it because her mother always had. Sophie called her grandma.

'Grandma, why did you cut the corners off your cake?' asked Sophie.

'My cake tin was square, but my cake box was round,' she explained. 'I had to cut off the corners so it would fit.'

Sophie had plenty of cake boxes, in a variety of shapes, as did her mother. For years, both had been following a process based on a truth that no longer held.

We're all guilty of cutting the corners off our cakes without asking why.

We don't always operate based on our own considered thoughts and actions. Perhaps you agreed to an opportunity because you were flattered someone wanted you involved, even though it distracted from your primary goal. Do you spend your evenings watching some show you don't like because you don't want to miss out? Maybe you didn't go out with someone who asked you on a date because of what a friend thought of them. Or you're with someone because of what your parents think of them.

Think back to the last time you did something without thinking for yourself about it. If you're very honest, that time was very recent – perhaps today. The truth is we all act, to some extent, based on unquestioned beliefs and systems – beliefs about how we should spend our days or what our house should look like or where we should live. Beliefs about what is and isn't feasible and the way of the world.

Blindly following

Even when we think we're choosing for ourselves, we're not.

During a scene in *The Devil Wears Prada*, intern Andy (Anne Hathaway) sniggers as her colleague decides between two belts. To Andy, the belts look exactly the same. Her boss, powerful Miranda Priestly (Meryl Streep), head of the fashion magazine *Runway*, sees the snigger and begins a calm attack on Andy's outfit. She asserts that while Andy thinks she indifferently selected the shapeless blue jumper she wears, actually, the specific blue shade was created, iterated and marketed by designers, editors and members of the fashion elite. While Andy, she says, might feel that all this fashion talk is beneath her, her sweater decision was made by the people in this room. Andy's smile vanishes.

You might think that you're smarter than that. You might think that your unbiased opinion and reasoned choice govern everything you think and do. But are you sure?

You chose your high school subjects. The university you went to, your college major. The graduate scheme you completed or the job you joined after graduating. You chose them all yourself.

Except you didn't.

They chose you. You saw a predefined set of options and picked one of them.

University marketing budgets are huge. Each government has quotas to hit. You are a number in a box on a spreadsheet that becomes a number in another box on another spreadsheet. You travelled the path expected of you. And why wouldn't you? Everyone else was doing it.

People often ridicule school dropouts, but they may be the only ones who understand.

The problem isn't only school. We are led to follow blindly in every aspect of our lives. You think you're choosing what you want, but you're not.

Consider what you eat. Menu psychology determines how to format a restaurant menu to maximize profit. It's a science. Best practice says that the most expensive item should be in the top right corner, because that's where a customer's eyes go first. This is where to put the mixed grill or the lobster – the obnoxiously expensive item that makes the others look cheap in comparison, with huge profit margins. It's there for show, but the restaurant wins if someone orders it.

There should be no currency symbols on a compelling menu. Currency symbols make prices look too much like money. Even better, round prices to one or no decimal places to extend the dissociation and encourage a higher spend. Don't line prices up. Instead, align them to the end of each dish title so they are harder to compare.

There's more. The wine with the highest profit margin is the second cheapest wine on the list. Menu creators know that guests avoid the house wine for fear of looking stingy. The one after that is the most popular, but its cost price is less than the house option. Then there's the music. The restaurant where I worked through sixth form played a specific CD during service. The title: 'Music to watch customers buy'. The songs were about treating yourself and your date, about indulgence, lavishness and having a great time. The songs rewired customers' brains to a more frivolous channel.

Department stores take people around the longest journey possible, so they see more products. Impulse purchases are next to the till. Then there's subliminal pairing. Ever arrived at the cinema only to crave popcorn? Of course you have. Popcorn, served in cinemas, is the globally recognized symbol for watching a film. You buy popcorn because that's what people do at movies. Do you still think it's your choice?

If you explained the concept of a mortgage to an alien, they would think you were crazy for even considering it. Yet we take mortgages for granted. Our rewired brains think that a mortgage is a great idea. Everyone else is doing it, so surely it's fine. But is it? If the caption 'We've signed for 35 years of debt' accompanied pictures of happy new homeowners holding keys, the sentiment might be different.

In 2020, during the Covid-19 lockdown, the number of dogs purchased soared. Google searches for 'buy a puppy' increased by 120 per cent in the first month of lockdown. 'Adopt a puppy' searches rose by 133 per cent, according to the UK charity Dogs Trust. People were at home; walking was one of the only reasons to venture out. Everyone else seemed to have a dog. There were pictures on social media of families buying one, reinforcing it as a good idea. Dogs are good for Instagram likes.

The dogs were happy, but were the people? When reality sunk in and they realized they had been keeping up with the Joneses instead of making their own choices, what happened? In the months following the spike in adoption, Dogs Trust received a record number of calls about rehoming dogs. If we don't think about our decisions, we will regret them.

If you are going to build a Ten Year Career, begin with understanding what to think about – perhaps something you have never examined – and how to think about it.

An indoctrination process is at play for much of life that we take for granted. Inception comes first; introduction of the concept followed by the subtle messaging that it is a good idea. Then comes awareness. Suddenly you see that purchase you toyed with everywhere. It must be a sign! Then we see others making that decision, which reinforces our plans – so we make them, too. Social media adds a new level of awareness and means trends can spread beyond local friendship groups or workplaces and across the world.

This works not only with purchases but with life events and how we assume they should be. The marketing tells us one thing – but it might not be true. Moving house does not have to be stressful. You don't need to own a television. You can have breakfast at any time of day. You don't have to binge in December and detox in January. You can make resolutions whenever feels right. If something has gone out of fashion, you can still wear it. Wiring happens everywhere. Department store ads tell us what a mother or a father should look like. Or a fun picnic. Or a Christmas dinner.

When a life decision, purchase or way of acting seems the normal thing to do, many will do it without questioning. Humans naturally want to stay away from danger, a proclivity that has been used to condition us to conform and not question. We are rewired to blindly follow.

Ask: *who is persuading us to do what, and why? Who creates the truth?* You do. Or you can, with enough intention.

If we assume that each person is holding at least a few beliefs that don't serve them, if finding safety in numbers and going along with a crowd become second nature, where does that lead?

Where it leads

Imagine viewing your city from a height. You would see thousands of people going about their day, following linear paths. They travel the same ups and downs as everyone else, and they hardly question the way.

Harry arrived on his first day at my agency ready to get cracking. His CV was strong, and he got good grades at school. He had a bit of work experience and came across well during his interview. He negotiated a higher starting salary because his mum told him he should. The negotiation had worked, and here he was: overpaid, overdressed and ready to begin.

Harry could follow a process diligently. He did his best work when it was a series of tasks accompanied by clear instructions. He didn't think outside tick box tasks and would keep doing the same thing even when results suggested a change in method. Unless someone else, a manager or colleague, provided the new direction, Harry followed the same route to little avail. He kept on ticking his tasks. He was a human nodding dog.

Harry would gauge work by its difficulty: difficult was bad and easy was good. If difficult things cropped up, Harry ignored them until they went away. He didn't like talking to clients with probing questions, scrapping a campaign and starting again, or testing a new way forward. He would make difficult things someone else's problem. He'd move towards easy wherever possible but fail to see that it was limiting his potential and narrowing his comfort zone.

In discussions about improving, Harry would point to the stressful time he was having outside work: moving to a new house, transitioning to a new job, having to wake up earlier. We couldn't rely on Harry for anything other than following a set process to defined standards. Where could he have learned that?

The beliefs and systems that shaped Harry were not set up so he, or you, could maximize potential and live a dream life. They serve another purpose, and it starts with schooling.

Harry is not a bad person. Harry is a product of the education system, intelligent and great on paper but not fit for purpose, other than for a production line or factory work. The opposite of resourceful, Harry needs a teacher and a mark scheme. He wants to progress along a linear route in his career, against defined standards, and attributes lack of progress to each employer. He waits for each line manager to provide the answers and change his destiny. Harry job-hops, looking for an easier way to make his mark, and will continue taking side steps in his career until he has an epiphany or a midlife crisis. We're all a bit of Harry sometimes.

The schooling system creates people like this. It's set up for people to follow instructions, follow rules and secure standard, safe jobs. But clerical roles and those involving following simple processes are declining in number. Automation is replacing so many jobs that adaptability and creativity are the most important skills to hold.

Author Seth Godin would call Harry a cog. A cog in a wheel, 'standing by, waiting for instructions'. Schooling can reduce progression to tick boxes, but the jobs of today cannot, and neither can entrepreneurship. 'Your ability to follow instructions,' Godin writes, 'is not the secret to your success.'

Online learning platform Udemy has courses that explain how to start or grow a business. These courses, of which there are thousands, provide theory, case studies and step-by-step breakdowns. There are formulae for choosing a business idea, email templates to copy, and guidance on how to do every aspect of running a business. The one-star reviews of any given course speak volumes. Bad reviews don't mention production quality or presenter style. Instead, they blame the course for not spoon-feeding. 'Wasn't relevant to my business', 'Didn't result in sales', 'Didn't understand how to do it' are phrases that come up repeatedly. Participants expect the presenter to play the role of a teacher, providing the curriculum and the mark scheme, and teaching everything required to grow a successful business. When that doesn't happen, it's the course creator's fault. The student didn't want to figure anything out for themselves. They've never had to so far.

But that doesn't work, and it can never work because entrepreneurship can't be spoon-fed. No two journeys are the same. There is no fixed path to success. It requires critical and intentional thinking at every stage.

Those who use the material as inspiration and guidance but apply their own enthusiasm and imagination do well, but they would have done well anyway. Those who follow but don't think, not realizing thinking is required, wind up frustrated and resolve to leave a bad review. The latter is all too common.

The root cause

An education conveyor belt exists, and it's likely you've been through it. It starts with enrolling at primary school and moves on to secondary school and college. We learn how to stay in line, follow a curriculum and pass exams. We pick from a finite set of options for how we'll spend the following few years, and that keeps happening. We think we are in control, but it's an illusion.

Schools cater for the slowest moving. They split pupils into sets based on ability. People learn in different ways but are all taught using the same methods. Every student is graded against the same standards based on what they can recall for an exam paper. It's normal, so we believe it's right.

Author John Taylor Gatto, who taught in New York schools for 30 years, thinks schooling does more harm than good. The problem is not just what is taught, it's how: 'School trains children to be employees and consumers; teach your own to be leaders and adventurers. School trains children to obey reflexively; teach your own to think critically and independently.' Instead we conform and toe the line and don't realize what's happening. How did you learn to be a leader and adventurer? How did you learn critical thinking and independence? Probably not from schooling; that education came elsewhere.

Most establishments are likely doing the best they can within a web of standards. Schooling teaches students how to pass exams because that's how schools are assessed. Colleges prepare students to get a job because that's how colleges are assessed. A curriculum consists of subjects, and subjects consist of levels. Students learn the levels in turn, assessed via exams. The exams measure ability levels against a mark scheme. The school year teaches students about a subject according to what will be on the exam. Students sit the exam, regurgitate knowledge, and then forget.

In the mess of curricula, mark schemes and governing bodies, questioning and thinking for ourselves are schooled out of us. The damage is twofold. First, we teach young people to obediently follow orders and do the minimum required to pass exams. Second, we define success as passing tests for which you knew exactly how to prepare. Independence and resourcefulness are not required to pass through this system. Whether you develop that depends on other factors.

Pushing everyone along a one-size-fits-all route doesn't create independent and resourceful people. It's not what sets up happy and successful futures.

Humans choose pleasure and avoid pain, but most coast in the middle doing enough to stay out of trouble but not enough to make a change. It can take something drastic to create a realization that leads to progress, either consistent inspiration or a moment of sheer desperation that creates growth. Or, you can develop the discipline to choose change without a crisis. That's how you build a Ten Year Career.

The normal route will keep you blending in and playing small. It's not easy to realize what's happening or step away from it because it's normalized among groups. Office politics. Water cooler conversations. Playing games. If you let them, they will keep you aiming low and not standing out too much. But blending in and going with a crowd isn't where the magic happens.

Going with the crowd can look different from what you expect. You might think you are breaking away when you aren't. I once interviewed someone named Max. I asked him about his plans, and he told me that he wanted to work at an agency and then start his own. Impressed with his ambition, I had many questions. *How exciting, Max! What type of agency will you start? Who will your clients be?*

Max didn't know. Max didn't know because he planned to start his agency when he had ten years of working for others under his belt. I had more questions. *Why ten years? Why not now? What did he hope to gain from the experience of work that would mean he could start up alone?* It turned out Max had seen a statistic on the average age of people who started a business that became a success. He had decided that was when he would start his, and he had ten years to kill before then.

Once you start breaking away, there will be resistance. You will be doing what many others don't have the courage to do. You will stand out and appear different and they might feel threatened. Yet you'll find fans and champions along with haters and naysayers.

The old model isn't relevant anymore. Things change faster now. This is not a dress rehearsal and we're not going to live for ever. The goal is not to punch keys on a computer until we die. There is another way.

Thinking for yourself

By my third year of university I was itching to finish. I felt like I was in limbo, waiting for real life to start. Yet when I graduated, I didn't know what to do, so I took the next logical step and enrolled on a graduate scheme with the UK's National Skills Academy (NSA) for Social Care, set up to create the next wave of social care leaders.

Each person interned at a social care organization for a year. The NSA, rather than the host, paid our wages, and every two months we attended a two-day cohort-wide intensive leadership course. Here we brought challenges and observations from our workplaces for discussion. We were also assigned a business coach to work with throughout the year.

Combining challenging work experience with personal development created leaders in social care every year that the scheme was in place. It worked because we learned how to question. Only recently did I come to appreciate how fortunate I was to have an intense programme of personal development that so few entrepreneurs have at the start of their journey.

Some of the host organizations had been operating in the same way for 30 years but were being forced by the market to adapt, something our fresh perspectives could help with. When we faced resistance from our host organizations, we had support networks with whom to work through challenges. We discussed the possibilities and shared our experiences with 24 other people. We were taught empathy and persuasion in a work context, so we could sell our ideas back to our host organizations.

The two-day courses included group coaching, personality tests and critical thinking exercises most 21-year-olds had never heard of. We took the personality tests so we could understand ourselves better. We interrogated our strengths and weaknesses and discovered our preferred working style. This was the foundation from which we built. Critical thinking exercises established us as the drivers of our careers, not the other way around. The NSA gave us permission to unpack and question authority and longstanding processes. Having been through normal schooling up to that point, such behaviour wasn't second nature to any of us.

The group coaching method, in which we split into groups of four or five and took turns bringing a problem or challenge to the group, was uncomfortable at first. I would explain a specific challenge, and the others would ask me questions. They offered no advice or words of wisdom, just fired question after question that I had to answer. When I didn't have a good answer they kept pressing. Shoddy responses wouldn't cut it. I had to think and speak coherently with four sets of beady eyes on me, ready with their follow-ups. The group coaching meant that, although we were at identical stages in our careers, we could use each other as resources. Breakthroughs for some meant breakthroughs for all.

These and other one-to-one coaching sessions, which we had every month, allowed me to become an observer of my career rather than a passive cog in a wheel. I was becoming less of a worker bee and more of the queen. We all were. I watched, made notes, and tried to make sense of what I was learning. When I had a coaching session coming up, I became more aware of what was happening in my day-to-day, which was my material, my muse and my content for the sessions. When I felt like I hadn't been able to contribute to a meeting, I told my coach and we worked out why. I came away with a plan of how to be better at my job. When my boss said something I didn't understand, we'd unpack it and work out what they meant.

I felt like I was actively watching myself at work rather than bumbling along wishing the clock would hit 5 pm. I was present, aware and alert. The self-development sessions gave my week direction and my work a purpose.

By teaching us how to think, the scheme fast-tracked graduates into leadership positions, bringing welcome change to the social care sector.

One day I was talking with Glyn, my internship manager, about what I would do when my graduate scheme year was complete, and the hopes of the NSA for its cohort of social care management trainees. Glyn was quick to tell me, 'You're not going to walk out of here and be a manager. It's just not going to happen.' I wrote that down in my journal because I wasn't sure he was right. We had just learned of a concept called 'limiting beliefs', which are thoughts or opinions that someone believes to be an absolute truth. Glyn's assertion sounded suspiciously like one of those.

After analysing what he said, as I had been shown how to do, I realized that Glyn wasn't trying to be mean, he just didn't want me to face disappointment when I realized that the future was bleak. Glyn saw it as his role to set the record straight and make sure I was being realistic.

Glyn's limiting belief was that a graduate couldn't walk straight into a management role.

Someone's assessment of your capability is a reflection on them, not you.

It's a myth that you have to start at the bottom and work your way up. Starting at the bottom will trap you. It's a myth that you have to do your career steps in a prescribed order. The world is different now. It's a myth that you have to earn your stripes according to anyone else's definition other than your own. It's a myth that you can't go from education to world domination. You can.

My graduate scheme was a godsend. It was a programme that undid much of the damage of my traditional schooling up to that point because it taught me how to question and how to think. The elements of my graduate scheme that transformed my thinking for ever were:

- Personality and working style analyses, to understand myself
- Making regular notes in my notebook, to observe and later analyse
- One-to-one coaching sessions, to unpack challenges and question events
- Questioning within a group of individuals at similar stages, to see and think from a variety of perspectives
- Being encouraged to question both authority and the norm.

You can replicate each of these elements in your own life. Together they create a self-aware, confident, assertive and intentional way of operating. Together they set up a Ten Year Career.

Start a business when you suspect you can. Be a leader when you're inspired to lead. Grow your business when doing so is right for you. The standard pace is not your thing, and it never was. Where we are going, there is no mark scheme.

The Ten Year Career is unimaginable for someone conditioned to think in the old way, but thinking in a different way makes it possible. Something has to change, and this book is your start.

So what?

Most of the population follows outdated beliefs, finds safety in numbers, and goes along with a crowd. This way of getting along in the world is the backbone of schooling and continues throughout a career unless something changes.

Questioning everything won't be second nature, but it's necessary to have the life and career we want. Entrepreneurs aren't immune to conformity. We need to unpick the system we have become accustomed to, get intentional, and jump off the career conveyor belt.

Key takeaways

- Question your beliefs – are they outdated?
- Notice limiting beliefs when used by others.
- Ask yourself where you are blindly following or being led.
- Traditional education doesn't prepare you to thrive. It's a conveyor belt.
- 'Normal' keeps you playing small.
- Learn to think for yourself!

There's more

Head over to the free *Ten Year Career* companion course for short videos and bonus downloads to apply this chapter's concepts and frameworks to your life and business.
Find it at jodiecook.com/TYC

2

What's The Alternative?

● ● ●

Justin Woolverton, founder of HALO Top ice cream, created his product as an experiment in his Los Angeles home in 2011. He was good at marketing, he was into fitness and he wanted low-calorie desserts.

For years a few players had dominated the ice cream industry. Woolverton saw a gap they hadn't explored: low-calorie ice cream that tasted good. It didn't exist. Most ice cream contained dense fudge, chocolate pieces and calorific sauces. A tub could contain over 1,000 calories. Woolverton wanted to eat an entire tub in one sitting without feeling guilty, so he set about making it.

The big ice cream names he was up against could have intimidated Woolverton, but they didn't. Barriers to entry could have blocked his way: equipment, food safety, not to mention the fact that ice cream requires a certain temperature to make, store and transport. Most people wouldn't have even started, but Woolverton began playing around with ingredients in his kitchen. He weighed them, worked out the calories in each tub and wrote down recipes that tasted good.

In 2016 a *GQ* journalist wrote about how he had eaten only HALO Top ice cream for ten days straight. The witty article went viral and orders went crazy. A few months before, Woolverton had pleaded with supermarkets to keep his ice cream stocked when sales were too low to warrant the shelf space. He begged for a little longer. The brand worked hard to promote itself on social media, culminating in the *GQ* piece that changed everything.

That year, HALO Top sold 28.8 million tubs and became the best-selling ice cream in the US. In 2019 Justin sold the US arm of the business for an 'undisclosed amount'. An eight-year career. Right place, right time, right idea, done. The HALO Top founder spent eight years powering on with the idea he knew was going to be big.

This chapter is about the antithesis of a life lived according to lies. I'll explain how and why to question nearly everything, introduce you to people who have reimagined their work and life no matter their age or phase, and show how you can choose yourself instead of waiting in line to be picked. We'll explore why to swap passion for intention, look at strategies for seeing and creating the future, and explain how insane self-awareness underpins this journey. You'll understand how to ensure you are in control of your brain, rather than at the mercy of your thoughts, and redefine retirement to suit your plan.

Question everything

During a scene in *The Matrix*, the protagonist, Neo (Keanu Reeves), is waiting to meet The Oracle (Gloria Foster). He stands in a waiting room with other people, mainly children. One, with a shaven head and a monk's robe, holds a spoon and bends it purely with his intent. Neo looks confused.

The boy hands Neo the spoon and tells him not to try to bend the spoon, for that is impossible. Instead, Neo should try to realize the truth: that there is no spoon. The boy makes the distinction between bending the spoon and bending yourself. Neo stares at the spoon he holds. By following the boy's guidance, he is able to bend the spoon using only his mind.

The premise comes from Buddhist philosophy, which holds that logic is an inadequate path to enlightenment. The Oracle instructs Neo to let go of fear, doubt and disbelief, to open his consciousness to all that is possible. That action sets the entire plot in motion.

Everything about your career is up for questioning. You can bend the spoon, but not in the normal way. In living and thinking differently, you must be comfortable with being the weird one. Eccentric, unusual, kooky or odd, call it what you will. The world needs such people. If you're on the right lines, that's what you'll be called. If someone doesn't understand you, they will try to label you, and that's fine. You'll know the truth. There is no spoon.

If you are intentional about creating and following your own path, not led astray by others, you will be different. Very few reimagine their work. Not all business owners move beyond the comfort of what they know. But now is the best time to do it.

Reimagine your work

Reimagining your reality isn't limited to your work, but let's start there. To begin, understand there has been a fundamental shift of power across the economy, and this shift means enormous opportunities are opening everywhere. The gatekeepers of every industry are no longer in charge. They may think they are, but they sit on a ticking time bomb. They are being muscled out by ideas, technology and innovation, forced to operate differently or leaving of their own accord.

In years gone by, if I wanted to publish a book, my only choice would have been to find a publisher who would have me. I would research and approach publishers, only to hear rejections. It might have been possible to secure a deal, but only by finding the right person at the right time, with the right book. Finding that needle in a haystack might have taken a lifetime. I would call myself undiscovered and say that no one gave me a chance to share my work. I would complain that no one took a gamble on me.

Now, I can take the gamble myself. I can write my manuscript solo. I can hire help to create the perfect title and subtitle. I can hire a copyeditor and cartoonist and a panel of editors to scrutinize my work. Or I can learn how to do all these things for free on YouTube and call in favours for second opinions. I can add the manuscript to Amazon and hire a cover designer. I can learn graphic design and make my own cover. I can have my book ready for the world to buy within weeks. How far it goes, the marketing and hype I create, is up to me; but that was up to me anyway.

All kinds of excuses for not writing a book used to be available. Mystery shrouded the process, and swanky offices and tall closed doors guarded it. The method was a secret, and only insiders got in. Then the internet, globalization, the gig economy and Covid-19 came in turn and transformed how we work and what is possible. Now, there is no excuse. Publishing a book or making a success of any commercial venture relies on making a plan and sticking to it.

Street performers set up in busy city centres. Some amass an audience, some don't. They take the feedback of the crowd and they improve their act. They have a direct connection with their audience, who film their performances and distribute clips online. We are all street artists now. We need no one's permission to perform.

The pattern replicates in almost every industry. The platforms exist; it's up to individuals to use them. You can create anything you like and sell it on Etsy. YouTube is the global TV network where you can be the star. You can travel the world looking for curious objects to sell on eBay. You can leverage Alibaba and Amazon and make a killing. You can self-publish and self-produce. You can run your own membership organization or film courses, teaching others whatever you know.

Success is less about banging down doors and more about finding other options. It's more about building your own house of opportunities and having people knock on your door. In the meantime you may have found everything you need in your hallway. Instead of waiting to be picked, you can pick yourself.

One common mistake when starting or running a business is to look at what potential competitors are doing. It's far more powerful to completely ignore them. This can sound counterintuitive. What it does, though, is free you up to see possibilities. Refusing to acknowledge competitors of your business is a powerful play and it forces attention elsewhere. It keeps a business looking forward. There is no point gauging your progress by looking to others. Some of the best business owners I've met have no idea what their so-called competitors are doing. They don't copy those in the same industry; they look to other places for inspiration and ideas.

This is not the norm. But remember, you aren't trying to do what everyone else does. You are building a Ten Year Career. For many businesses, the norm is to obsess over their competition. They visit their websites, set up Google Alerts for their name, keep a close eye and copy strategies. It happens with local businesses and huge brands and keeps everyone playing small. Not only that, you give undue attention to a brand that isn't you, a brand your customers may never have heard of. Giving energy to your competition works on a scarcity mindset – that there isn't enough to go around. It assumes a zero-sum game. This isn't the case.

If you're looking for examples, stop. If you're looking for competitors, stop. If you're looking for some kind of blueprint on how to guarantee success, stop. All you will find is trodden paths and reasons not to do things. The success you're looking for exists within you – doing something you do well in a different way. You can join a crowd, or you can have the crowd join you.

It's never too late to start your Ten Year Career. You can begin straight out of school, after a few years of freelancing, or following a long stint in a slow-moving industry. What matters is it happens.

Anne Boden had a 30-year career in banking before she resolved to change the industry in 2014. She saw the potential for digital banking technology and made the app that started Starling Bank from scratch. She was 54. Now Starling Bank's CEO, she builds and leads the team, keeping change and speed at the heart of its mission. The bank has over 2 million customers and has raised over £360 million in funding. Boden still owns a quarter of the company.

Boden had picked up industry knowledge and had a dossier of changes she knew banks needed to make to keep up with technology. She compiled that dossier every day, learning from every experience, never settling into comfort. Doing her role well at each bank meant she created the space to think. She reimagined the future of a longstanding and rigid industry.

Picture your career as a game of 'Snakes and Ladders'. Perhaps, like Boden, you'll discover the existence of a board while you're do-ing other things. Boden was up for making real progress in financial services and she knew it would work. She saw her own playing field and she got onto it. Every day you roll the die and move forward on the board. Sometimes you hit a snake: a distraction, a big mistake, a loss in focus or a market shock. That might send you back a few spaces but you're still playing on the same board. Sometimes you hit ladders: chance encounters, dream opportunities, amazing ide-as, a market force that goes in your favour. Those ladders exist in every sector and every role, but most players have stopped rolling the die or they're inching along the board, unaware the ladders are even there.

Traditional career ladders might exist, but there's nothing to say you need to start at the bottom, whether your thing is ice cream, bank-ing or anything in between. Nothing governs how fast you can climb them. Nothing governs how many you can climb. The Goliaths are moving aside and the Davids are coming.

In *The Magic of Thinking Big*, author David J. Schwartz acknowl-edges the excuses people make as to why they can't do something such as be successful, grow their business or retire ahead of schedule. He says these people have 'excusitis'. Excuses range from 'I'm too old' to

'I'm too young' to 'I don't know enough' to 'I know too much'. Because their father was an alcoholic, because their father was rich, because their genes wouldn't let them, or they had tried before and it hadn't worked out.

Believing that you can't get started, or can't progress, because you need to learn the ropes, know industry players or have a bigger network is excusitis at play.

When we envision the reality we want – running our business with quadruple the clients while working from another country and spending our afternoons kitesurfing – it's easy to feel daunted. Rather than see a journey of incremental changes, we see one huge change and assume that everything has to happen at the same time. We see giant leaps, not baby steps. We freak out.

In reality, baby steps take us there. You won't suddenly wake up feeling that you know the ropes and can now progress your Ten Year Career. You move forward, and the ropes appear as string and twine before they build up. You won't suddenly feel you know the players in your industry sufficiently well to join them. You persevere with your work, and you become familiar with them one by one. You won't suddenly feel your network is large enough to launch a new concept. You meet people one event at a time and the network takes care of itself. Newton's first law states that objects in motion tend to stay in motion. In eating an elephant, you take one bite after the other. Your Ten Year Career is no different.

Fear of failure can also crop up as those 'what if?' questions creep in. What if I'm not good enough? What if I can't make it work? What if people laugh? What if I lose everything?

On the flipside of failure is huge success. What if it goes really well? What if my customers love my company? What if I make it work spectacularly? What if I achieve all my goals?

In response to fear of failure questions, the answer is, 'So what?' So what? Who cares? Does it really matter? Honestly, it probably doesn't. When you realize that your worst fears, upon coming to pass, wouldn't actually matter, going forward with big plans becomes the only option.

Once you decide to take action, the rest falls into place. The word 'decide' etymologically means 'to cut away'. Choosing and committing to your course of action means the nonessential falls away and the path appears.

Reimagine your life

Are you living to work or are you working to live? You're going down the route of entrepreneurship so you can craft the life you want to lead. Therefore, you need to scrutinize what that actually means.

Early one weekday morning I was listening to an interior designer tell networking event attendees about his work. On one slide he showed a home with a heat map of where its residents spent their time. Before the heat-mapping exercise, the family had sworn that they needed every inch of their home. But the heat map uncovered a different story.

They spent the majority of their time in specific spots in the living room and kitchen. They frequented the sink, toilet and shower areas, but that was about it. The heat map showed thoroughfares in use, such as hallways and stairs, but most of the house was only lightly visited.

They thought they needed space, so they bought it. Then they filled it. Now they needed it to hold their stuff. They would soon move to a bigger house and fill it with more stuff, each time tying their lives down to a specific location. The US transcendentalist writer Henry David Thoreau famously observed: 'A man is owned by his possessions.' From their house to the things that fill it, these people were enslaved by what they had.

Author Robert Kiyosaki, who wrote *Rich Dad, Poor Dad*, describes 'doo-dads' as things you buy that cost you money or waste your money. They might include luxury cars, jewellery or lavish clothes. In other words, anything that you don't need. There is a modern movement called minimalism, popularized by The Minimalists (US writers and podcasters Joshua Fields Millburn and Ryan Nicodemus), that advocates focusing on having less. Fewer possessions and fewer obligations. Less unimportant materialism and more spending time with people. Their mantra is 'love people, use things', because the opposite never works.

From a financial standpoint, every day of minimalism stacks up and could mean financial freedom is a whole lot closer. As Thoreau put it, 'My greatest skill has been to want little.'

There are two broad categories of lifestyle choice: 'settler' and 'explorer'. Settlers aim to settle. Their life's accomplishments tend towards security, including their career, location and family. Settlers are the target of most lifestyle marketing. Landing a dream role, signing for a gorgeous house, or finding a perfect partner, then a wedding and kids. Routines, contracts, long-term planning. Settlers are happy to have obligations and commitments that they work to sustain. While there is nothing wrong with being a settler, it's not for everyone.

The flipside is the explorer mindset. Explorers aren't fond of settling and prefer to regularly change their routine or have no routine. They are consistent travellers or avoid commitments that tie them down. They prize freedom over obligation and have high routine flexibility. They are low maintenance, adaptable and easy-going around change. Disorder and irregularity don't faze them, but long-term contracts and rigid commitments do.

Many settlers have a strong streak of explorer, so they keep as much freedom as possible within a settled foundation.

In a world aimed at settlers, explorers are different. Do you get itchy feet unless you're moving around or are you happy making home?

Before making any significant life choices, know who you are and what you want. Start with the essentials of what you need in your life and then go through every item or obligation and see if it fits. You might be surprised by how little you need and how much freedom that creates. Having less is a gateway to having more of what actually matters. Ask yourself: freedom from what, to do what?

Consider Katie McLeod. She travels the world with her family, updating her adventures on her blog and Instagram. Her online presence earns the family enough to live wherever they like. Dynamite Circle is an online community of 2,000 location-independent entrepreneurs. They live in condos, boats and vans, some by beaches or mountains, some in megacities, and all are open to learning from each other.

Would you want to do something like that? More and more, you can. An increasing number of countries are opening their borders and offering live and work visas to digital nomads, from one year to a lifetime. Moving to many countries is straightforward. You can if you want to.

There is nothing to say you have to live in a big city, or a house, or a fixed location. The year 2020 sped up the adoption of remote work and individualized ways of living by decades. Workers realized they didn't need to see each other to make progress and they figured a new way out, with help from those already doing it. I sold my social media agency without meeting any of the buyers face to face. What you want is possible wherever you are.

There are as many ways to live as there are people, yet 99 per cent live in the same way. What about your reality have you left unquestioned? Your town, your city, your country? How long you spend there? Whether you rent or buy? The true cost of your possessions?

Question everything.

Swap passion for intention

It is not my intention to show you how to start a business. If you've read this far, I know you either are committed to starting your own path or you already have a business but you want it to progress faster or better serve your life.

Like so much of what I recommend, the solution is paradoxical. We've all heard that we should 'do what you love' or 'follow your dream' or 'build your passion project'.

I disagree.

If you are going to build a successful Ten Year Career, swap the idea that you should do what you love for the idea that you should love what you do. Steven Pressfield, author of *The War of Art*, writes that this concept separates the amateurs from the professionals.

I call this swapping passion for intention. By 'intention', I mean that you make up for not knowing if you've found your calling by owning the space. I mean that you become the type of person who could sell anything. I mean that you become the type of person who any customer would trust and want to work with. I mean that you make whatever you choose to do your calling and use it to create your future.

When I started as a social media professional at age 22, social media was not my calling. I had no idea what my calling was; I hadn't even considered it. Instead of delaying action by overanalysing and overthinking, I got to work. I started down one route because I had enough of the right reasons to do so; it matched my skills, I thought it would be fun, and I had customers ready to buy.

My business served other businesses, so every day I met owners and marketing managers who did all sorts of work. Some companies sounded great: a national bouncy castle supplier, a meal delivery company, a sports protein brand. Some sounded boring as hell: insurance companies, car part fitters, a conference organizer. My naive self had expected the former to be bright, happy people and the latter dull and square. This wasn't the case. There was no correlation between how much someone enjoyed their work and the field they were in.

People get stuck because they are looking for their true calling or passion. That's a hidden excuse for inaction – self-sabotage at play. The people who loved their work found joy in what they did, regardless of their field. The owner of a corporate finance house wasn't fussed with numbers and deals; she loved nurturing teams. The owner of an insurance firm wasn't passionate about premiums; he wanted to protect people.

In an ideal world, you stumble upon something you love doing early. You find your calling. Work feels effortless and you attract amazing customers. Opportunities arrive from every direction, and your business grows. But life is not going to happen that way, and that's completely the wrong way to think about it. What you do doesn't matter. What matters is that you commit. Then what matters is that you excel at it.

What great businesses have in common is not how exciting their offering is, it's the intention of the team to make success happen. It's their shared ethos. They didn't feel as though they needed passion for the subject; they found their passion when they started down the route.

Your passion doesn't have to be confined to a specific role or industry. Your interest could be leadership, people or being exceptional. You can apply that to anything you do. Pick something. Pick anything.

Do what you're doing now but do it better. Find the way forward that no one else could. Reach a heightened sense of awareness in everything you do. Experiment. Mix it up. To create a Ten Year Career, you have to keep doing things differently than everyone else. Swapping passion for intention means taking a spark of interest and turning it into a plan. And the plan is a new plan, not the one everyone else is following.

In *The 4-Hour Workweek*, Tim Ferriss asked the question, 'What if I did the opposite?' for sales calls. Rather than making his calls between 9 am and 5 pm, he made them between 8–9 am and 5–6 pm. This meant he reached the decision-makers when their assistants weren't there. By doing the opposite, he found that the exact person he needed to speak to often answered the phone. It turned a monotonous, all-day sales process into a fun experiment that paid off.

Grant Cardone is a promoter of the 10X Rule to shake up thinking. Used almost to excess in Silicon Valley, it's a powerful way to remind yourself to think bigger. Not only bigger, but faster. Think of something you're doing right now and scale it up by a factor of ten. How would you do it? It could be securing ten times more orders for your product. Registering ten times the attendees for your webinar. Multiplying your mailing list subscribers by ten. Opening 20 more shops. Releasing 30 more flavours or colours or designs.

You might have preconceptions about what's feasible within a given space of time. If you apply the 10X Rule to time and achievement and force yourself to think about the how, the unknown becomes known. Once you know it, you can find a way to it.

The trick is to think ten times bigger while also delivering ten times more value. If serving ten times more customers means each one has a ten times worse experience, that's not progress.

Get out of your lane

Author David Epstein, when researching generalists and specialists, found that progress in many fields, including science, occurs at the interfaces. He found that scientists with a narrow specialty often missed opportunities to make breakthroughs that required wider knowledge. This is where generalists thrive. They can grasp the structure of a concept and find similar structures from other fields. They can use analogies to explain a solution or find a way forward. They bring a wide field of knowledge to narrow ones and come up with ideas that seem wacky but are actually genius.

The interfaces between two fields are where those unexplored opportunities lie. Those opportunities can create important building blocks for a Ten Year Career. In practice, this means looking to other industries for answers.

For instance, I found an insight for my social media agency in the gym business. When I started my agency, I began signing clients for a fixed monthly fee. I researched how I should structure payments.

The print and promotion office I had worked in charged upon delivery of the products – after doing the work. Other marketing firms invoiced clients at the end of each month, with 30-day terms. I wasn't sure these ways of working were very good. In the marketing agency case, day one's work wasn't paid until 60 days later, and that was if the client paid on time.

Realizing that the way professional marketing firms charged was not ideal, I looked for other models. I looked outside my industry. I thought about what else is paid in monthly instalments and hit upon gym membership and rent. Gym membership and rent are due, in full, at the start of your month with the gym or the property, often by direct debit.

When onboarding clients I began to stipulate that payment was due by the first day of each month. I included a link to set up a direct debit. My onboarding email became a template, along with a template of FAQs on why we charged up front and required direct debit for our services. In 2011 advance billing wasn't common practice, so I prepared for pushback. I received none. No client questioned paying up front, and 80 per cent signed our direct debit mandate upon receiving setup instructions. The rest preferred to pay by bank transfer and we let them as long as they promised to do so on time.

Now common practice, at the time mine was a new way of working in my industry. Copying the strategies of competitors would have meant payments became an unnecessary hassle. The answer came from the interfaces – in seeing how gyms and landlords charged. What could you put into place now that will, one day, be common practice?

While this way of thinking might come naturally, we can't leave it to chance. Pick a few industries to keep abreast of. Research new inventions or breakthroughs and find out how they were discovered. Or ask a friend in a different field about their work. The ways they solve problems might well apply to your future ones. Intentionally learning from other fields doesn't require passion. Intentionally thinking bigger doesn't need to either.

See the future

In September 2000 Netflix made $35.89 million in sales but total net losses increased to $58.27 million – the highest since its inception. Blockbuster, meanwhile, had completed a successful initial public offering and raised $465 million the previous year. Netflix asked video rental chain Blockbuster to buy the company for $50 million, but the Blockbuster CEO didn't consider it. He dismissed the proposition, believing that their customers would always want to go out and select a film from a physical store.

Blockbuster found out they were wrong soon after. Blockbuster's predictions of the future were what they wanted to happen, not what would happen. They filed for bankruptcy in 2010. Meanwhile, in March 2022 Netflix's market cap was $163.19 billion.

In order to access new levels in a business, don't simply wait to see how things unfold. By then, the rest of the world has had a chance to respond. One way to succeed faster is by being better at predicting the future and capitalizing on it.

Opportunity can be found in the darkest scenarios. In March 2020 the UK went into national lockdown in a bid to stop coronavirus case numbers from rising. As part of the lockdown, many shops, restaurants and bars had to close. This was widely seen as disastrous.

Lydia Papaphilippopoulos owns two coffee shops in the Midlands, which closed their doors. At the same time, she joined a WhatsApp group for hospitality owners within her city. As time under lockdown passed, she found the members split into two camps. Eighty per cent of members, although not happy that their venues had to close, saw lockdown as a short break during which they expected to recharge, let case numbers fall, then reopen. That was the future they wanted to see. The other 20 per cent weren't convinced. The lockdown duration had been loosely specified as one month, but what if it was longer?

After looking into how other countries responded and how global viruses had affected the world in years gone by, Lydia sprang into action. She decided to prepare for lockdown to extend throughout the entire year. She spent long days alone in both shops, working out how she was going to pull this off. She predicted the future, concluding that even if case numbers fell, customers sitting inside her coffee shops would be a long way off. Where, she thought, was the opportunity?

During the first lockdown she organized a delivery service for her shops and reorganized the floor plan to serve customers from a hatch, rather than inside. Before closing, the shops had served flatbreads piled high with toppings. Those wouldn't transport well on delivery bikes, so she organized Zoom meetings with her chefs and they planned food that wouldn't spoil when taken away.

She didn't stop there. Lydia set up a Shopify site to take online orders. Her chefs worked out meal boxes for collection or delivery. The meal boxes had themes, and she released a new one every week. Each release went out to their mailing list and then to social media. The list grew. Lydia planned shifts so her chefs worked solo to minimize their contact with others.

By March 2021 the UK was in its third lockdown. The WhatsApp group members were lobbying the government for funding and announcing permanent closures. Country-wide, 72 per cent of hospitality businesses expected to close their doors; meanwhile Lydia's coffee shops were earning more revenue than they had before the global pandemic and she has since opened a third venue. That success took planning, hard work and a bit of luck, but by adapting early to the future she saw, not the future she (and her fellow restaurant owners) wanted, Lydia was able to thrive.

You can see the future and adapt to it. Or you can make the future if you spot the right opportunity.

Jeff Bezos, founder of Amazon and one of the richest people of all time, enjoys predicting what might happen. Then he goes and makes it happen (contrast this to the leadership at Blockbuster, which tied the company to what they wanted to happen). When he launched Amazon in July 1995, Bezos's vision was for an online store that sold everything anyone could need. Bezos started with books because buyers don't need to touch or feel them before purchase and they were standardized. His passion wasn't books – he didn't spend hours in bookstores or have a penchant for libraries – but they made the most sense as a starting point.

After Amazon changed the book industry, it moved on to kitchenware. But the legacy of selling books lingered in the system. For a while every new product added to Amazon's computers required categorizing as fiction or non-fiction. The delivery chutes down which books would fly, ready for shipping, now hurled out unboxed kitchen utensils including sharp knives.

Amazon was paving the way for the future Bezos pictured, and he didn't slow down. Kitchenware led to homeware and electronics and other categories. Bezos believed that clothes and food were the pinnacle; whoever cracked those categories would be the winner who took all. He predicted that the online store that sold everything would be the biggest store in the world, and he turned out to be right.

How do you see into the future? Start small. Think about everything you do regularly and how you might do it one day. Think of how consumer trends, technology, the economy, free or restricted movement of people might change everything.

Digging into every eventuality gives insights into how we will live and work. Patterns, habits, wants and needs dictate what businesses will offer. Predict the future that is coming and adapt to it. Or see the future you want to build and then create it. Doing this exercise might mean you hit upon your exact place in this reality. You might know exactly what you need to do.

Self-awareness

How would your actions change if you knew someone was observing and narrating your every move? While this might sound creepy, knowing that someone is watching brings awareness because we see our actions through someone else's eyes. It might mean we act like the best versions of ourselves. We show the side we want people to see. How do you act when you suspect someone is watching?

Imagine you are watching two people, narrating what you see:

Luke is sitting on the sofa with crumbs down his jumper. He's flicking through channels to decide what to watch. He gazes over to the mess piling up in the kitchen. He picks up his phone to distract himself from the work he should be doing.

Nic is making coffee. She picks it up and walks over to her desk. She is now sitting at her laptop. She is opening a Word document. She is getting ready to work on her manuscript. She stretches up and takes a deep breath in, then exhales and begins typing. She is so engrossed in her work that she doesn't hear the doorbell until the third ring. She gets up to see who's outside.

Now imagine doing this for yourself. What would you say? How would it sound to hear someone describe what you do every day, week, month, year? Does that story make you cringe a little bit? This is a powerful exercise through which you can gain insight into how the hardwiring in your brain is helping or hurting your progress towards a Ten Year Career.

Our brains can be imagined as having three functional sections: the visionary part, the routine part and the amygdala, responsible for what is known as the 'lizard brain'. The visionary part, when in charge, means we are creative and forward-thinking. We can plan ahead and feel excited about the possibilities. We can dream big about what's possible and feel as if our capability has no limits.

The routine brain rules when we're doing those tasks that we have done thousands of times before, in exactly the same way. You might not have realized you brush your teeth exactly the same way every day until your dentist points out the spot you always miss.

Many aspects of school require the routine part of the brain to be in charge. Lining up, answering to a register, passing your exams. Many more careers used to – for example, clerical and factory work that meant diligently following instructions.

The third part is the amygdala, which incorporates the lizard brain. This is the part responsible for fight or flight. It's in charge of fear. It wants everything to stay the same because it views change as scary, and it will invent excuses and stories to ensure a stable footing. The lizard brain is scanning for danger and worrying about what might lie ahead. It's battening down the hatches, double-checking you locked the door, and trying not to draw attention for fear of undesirable consequences. It's triggered by the nightly newscast. It never sees the opportunity in disruption or imagines a better future.

Once you obey the lizard brain, it feels safe. It reassures its owner that they made the right choice. It might recall examples of people who went too far and failed. Thank goodness that wasn't you, it will say. The lizard brain holds us back. It keeps us from creating, sharing and putting ourselves out there. It avoids change and risk.

The lizard brain is you at your worst. It's you when you're cranky, tired, hungry. When you're bursting for the toilet. When you snap at someone or when an innocent comment leads to an overreaction. When you make excuses for why you shouldn't take that leap or make that call or publish that article.

If left unchecked, anything can move someone's thinking to the lizard brain way. One email might have the power to change their entire mood. One loud noise, a piece of news coverage. Something being put back in a different place. A waiter not writing down an order. The more self-aware you become, the more you realize which part of your brain is running the show.

The lizard brain creeps up on us; it's our job to tame it. If I'm feeling tired or hungry, if I haven't been outside that day or am feeling uninspired, I can sense myself slipping into a fear-based mentality. The faster I can notice and change it, the better I will become at leading my life from the best version of myself. Training your amygdala to be less reactive leads to more resilience and less stress.

Life coach Gabrielle Bernstein advocates her 'choose again method' for moving from fear to love, an approach that leaders can incorporate into their day. The steps include:

- noticing your negative or fearful thought
- forgiving the thought
- recognizing the role of undesirable thoughts in showing you what you actually want
- choosing again, with the best alternative feeling you can muster.

In practice, choosing again stops the spiral of negative thoughts and helps a leader move from fear to love. It means reframing a busy calendar as a chance to meet amazing people. Uncertainty about a team member's work becomes a chance to talk them through what's expected and hear their ideas for change. A difficult conversation with a supplier becomes an opportunity to find a better solution. When you consciously begin to follow the choose again process, it starts to come naturally.

When I feel my lizard brain leading, I don't talk to anyone. I know that not every word I say will be true to who I am and what I know. I don't let the lizard send emails, make decisions or think about the future. Instead, I choose again. I do anything possible to put myself back into a visionary mindset before my low energy transfers to someone else or projects onto the future. Only then do I engage in making plans or involving others. When we are angry, it's almost always better to wait and do nothing.

What are your lizard brain triggers? Perhaps you feel lethargic at the same time every day because you always have the same big lunch. Or you get frustrated every Christmas Day because an uncle says something abrasive. Or get annoyed whenever you go to that restaurant that always messes up your order.

The last few hours before bed, if not protected, are prime moments when your lizard brain may reign. Letting it be in charge can mess up sleep. It can cause needless worry before resting and can throw out your next day. Consuming media after dark is a guaranteed way to wake your lizard up, ready for worry. Don't do it. Instead, narrate your own life.

Self-awareness is far too important to not master. Bad decisions are made under the influence of the lizard brain. If it's controlling your actions, your best self is not.

A self-aware career

The big jobs go to those who prove their ability to outgrow the small ones.

Ralph Waldo Emerson, transcendentalist writer

During the last three years I owned my social media agency, Joanna managed the show. She kept a document on her desktop with the title 'Improvements'. She opened and updated it every day. If Joanna found herself unable to answer a question well or didn't know what to do in a scenario, she made a note. Every few weeks, when we caught up, Joanna and I went through the additions. She asked questions about alternative ways she could have phrased her words or handled a situation. I asked her questions and told her what I thought. I referenced articles or books she could read and gave suggestions on concepts to check out. She always did.

This exercise wasn't part of her job description, but Joanna was hell-bent on being the best version of herself. She wanted to excel in her role. She wasn't limited by her current self; she was always improving, always learning. She learned new ways of introducing topics or phrasing things and wrote them down. She learned frameworks that changed how she thought, spoke and managed. Today she holds shares in the group that purchased my agency, and her role has progressed to include managing many of its operations.

Knowing what you're good at and where you need work is the difference between the current and future versions of you. Your level of self-awareness is proportionate to your rate of improvement and progress.

Improving at record pace, as Joanna did, removes the need to follow the pace set by others. You fast-track progression and it's clear to you and others what is happening. Constant and rapid improvement is the key to growing out of the small jobs and into your Ten Year Career. Your work becomes your chosen path, not the default one. Along the route of improvement your value goes up, and you know exactly how to draw that value out to fund your life. Your financial needs are met and options open. You unlock a new level, where you focus on purpose and feeling good, rather than reimbursement. Your actions bring autonomy and freedom. In some ways, could this be considered as your being retired?

Redefine retirement

Most people don't think about what they want their future to look like until they're too far down one path. Many never get round to designing their life, career or even their weekend. But the earlier you make your plan, the sooner you can make progress or the sooner you can iterate.

Retirement once meant completely stopping work after a long career. We spend 'the best part of one's life earning money in order to enjoy a questionable liberty during the least valuable part of it,' wrote Henry David Thoreau. Now, it can mean achieving financial freedom; taking money out of the equation and pursuing whatever you please, which might be work but doesn't have to be.

Financial freedom or financial independence have become buzzwords in personal growth forums. The concept has many definitions. For me, financial freedom is about choice. Choosing who to work with, on which projects, from wherever in the world you want to be. It also means being able to say no to anything other than work that fulfils your mission and purpose, and yes to those opportunities that aren't necessarily well paid but are exciting.

You win at life when you are paid to do work that you love so much you'd do it for free. An extension of this is not having to work but believing so strongly that you're on to something that working is how you choose to spend your time.

The FIRE movement

The FIRE movement (financial independence, retire early) provides specific calculations to work out where you are versus where you want to be. The premise is to set aside 25 times your annual living expenses and put it into investments. It's not for everyone, but the concept is solid: work out where you are and work out what you need to do. Without an idea of how much you earn and how much you spend, it's impossible to plan ahead. Start with a blank piece of paper and work out your numbers. Use a banking app to analyse your spending. Get good at spreadsheets and, they advise, open a Vanguard account and put your money into index funds.

The mentality that 'a penny saved is a penny earned' is based on a scarcity premise and isn't congruent with the mindset of big thinkers or ambitious people. Alongside thinking of costs, think of opportunities. Think of the value you could bring to others and the financial rewards gained as a result. Incorporate that into your forecasts.

Scarcity mentality means you believe there isn't enough to go around. You believe that having more means someone else has less. For someone to win, someone has to lose. Scarcity implies a zero-sum game. It encourages holding your cards close to your chest, looking to take rather than give, and preserving what you have over looking for more.

Abundance mentality means you believe there is plenty to go around and that if I help you, we all win. Abundance mentality encourages openness, giving, sharing and spreading good vibes without keeping score. There is always a way of making more money or finding opportunities. There are chances to do so everywhere, but only if you think with an abundance mindset.

Believing in abundance changes your energy and brings a ripple effect. Without expectation of return, you receive favours and support. Opportunities are presented, doors open, miracles seem to happen. Your aura is one of happiness and love, and it attracts the same. You might think what I describe sounds fluffy, but I invite you to try operating from a place of abundance. You may be pleasantly surprised.

Abundance thinking stops the lizard brain in its tracks. Fear, anger and scarcity cannot exist alongside gratitude and abundance. The former brings misery; the latter attracts only good.

Retirement does not have to mean winding down or gardening and playing golf. It doesn't need to mean staying put and watching the days go by. Retirement means doing what you love and loving what you do. You might be working, because you love every aspect of it and you're in control of how you spend your time. 'Independence, to me, doesn't mean you'll stop working,' explained venture capitalist and author Morgan Housel. 'It means you only do the work you like with people you like at the times you want for as long as you want.'

Reimagine how you define retirement. It's about living a phase of life that is all on your terms, distinguished by its choice and freedom. Like Walt Disney, who said, 'We don't make movies to make money, we make money to make more movies,' you might have a mission to fulfil and an audience to serve, and financial reimbursement is a happy by-product of the value you bring. You might be in the top 1 per cent of earners because you deliver value to people who want more of it, but you're not dependent on the money and it doesn't define you.

With a heightened sense of self-awareness and your reality reimagined, you might find that the work you do starts not feeling like work. It might feel more like playing a fun game. Couple this with thinking bigger and going after bigger wins. Just as you've done with your career and your lifestyle and your future, you've made retirement what you want it to be. Not what someone else says it should be.

Keep reimagining your reality, your career, your life, your retirement. I hold that Matrix scene of the boy with the spoon at the forefront of my mind. Whenever there seems to be only one way forward. Whenever someone frets about what a perceived competitor is doing. Whenever I hear a situation described as hopeless by someone else.

Nothing is what it seems which means the possibilities are wide open. Whenever I load weight onto a bar before a heavy lift – at all of these moments, I remember that the spoon does not exist.

Next, let's get deeper into questioning everything and figure out just what you're capable of.

Key takeaways

- Everything about your career and life is up for questioning because there is no spoon.
- An economy-wide power-shift has opened enormous avenues of self-invention and recreation.
- To have something different, do something different. Ignore the competition. See the opportunity in disruption. Imagine the future you want.
- Reimagine your lifestyle.
- Don't do what you love, love what you do. And be great at it.
- Get out of your lane. Look for opportunities in unexpected places.
- Narrate your own life.
- Manage your lizard brain.
- Drive your own pace of improvement to get the jobs you want, not the jobs you're given.
- Define retirement to be what you want it to be.

Don't forget

Head over to the free *Ten Year Career* companion course for short videos and bonus downloads to apply this chapter's concepts and frameworks to your life and business.
Find it at jodiecook.com/TYC

3

What Are You Capable Of?

● ● ●

A young Oprah Winfrey watched her grandma pulling clothes pins from her apron and holding them two at a time in her mouth. She placed the pins on opposite ends of the sheets, towels, shirts and dresses she hung on the washing line in the yard. Her grandma had piles of clothes to hang, and some still boiling in a big black cast-iron pot.

Oprah was born in Mississippi in 1954, at a time when opportunities for black girls were limited. Her options were to be a maid, cook, dishwasher or servant. She could teach, but only in a segregated school.

Oprah was churning butter nearby when her grandma called out. 'Oprah Gail, you better watch me now, 'cause one day you gon' have to know how to do this for yourself.' As she walked over to watch her grandma hanging the washing, Oprah remembers the voice inside her. A still, small voice that said, 'No grandma, I won't.'

When recalling the story years later, Oprah explained, 'It's not that I've always known who I would be. It was just very clear to me from an early age who I wouldn't be.'

As you're reading this book, start to believe without a shadow of a doubt that great things are possible for you. When I talk about the incredible time you're going to have, I want you to feel without a doubt that what I describe is yours for the taking. You have to believe it in every bone of your body.

If you don't, it's because something else is at play:

- You've fallen into a normal way of living and you don't question enough.
- Or you hang out with the wrong people.
- Or something in your past is trying to own your future.

- Or you aren't sufficiently self-aware.
- Or you become distracted before making improvements.

Let this be the sign that something needs to change.

A journey of questioning

Before publishing my first business book, *Stop Acting Like You're Going to Live Forever*, in 2019, I read hundreds of articles of advice on publishing. I read two books on the topic that outlined the options available. They compared traditional, hybrid and self-publishing and gave advice for aspiring authors.

The authors were naysayers. The words 'You can't' started plenty of sentences. You can't just email your manuscript to a commissioning editor. You can't approach some publishers without an agent. You can't have control over the cover. If you're self-published, you can't be in bookshops. You can't secure translation deals.

Every time you hear 'you can't', read 'they can't'. The speaker of the words can't. The person hearing the words can always question. There is always a way.

The publishing books I read were managing expectations of their audience, showing them that writing and publishing your work is no mean feat. I chose to read every 'you can't' as: There's a way forward here, but only if you're determined. There's no formula for the way through the 'you can'ts', so there's no step-by-step guide to follow. There is no replicable way of succeeding, only replicable ways of failing. Every great success happens when someone questions rather than mimics. There is no mark scheme. No blueprint. No instructions to follow.

The person who has done it will say it's possible. Their way of doing it might no longer be relevant, it might have expired or been written into cheats and hacks. But the fact that they found a way of turning a 'you can't' into an 'I can' is the message that matters. The person who hasn't done it likely will say it isn't possible, but they're wrong.

Be intentional about the way you think by being intentional about what you share and with whom. If you can't find someone who has done something you want to do, find someone who believes in possibilities. Someone who is curious enough to think about how.

Someone who has already found a way around obstacles, can come up with ideas on the spot, or has a knack for being jammy. Jammy people can apply their thinking to any situation and are great to have in your life.

I can and I will

'No one's going to pay that,' smirked Pete.

I was about to start my social media agency, and I had told people too much too soon. Friend-of-a-friend Pete wanted me to halve my prices. 'It's far too much. Anyone can update their Facebook status; it's not rocket science. You can't charge that.' (I knew there was more to my work than updating statuses.)

'No one's going to pay that,' exclaimed Gary.

Gary was a top lawyer working in London and Silicon Valley. His clientele were tech CEOs and billionaire investors. 'It's far too cheap. No one will think you're serious. You need to have a bigger proportion of marketing budgets to make a difference. You need to double your prices.'

In 2011 there were very few social media agencies. There were very few social media freelancers. I was creating a set of services and their respective fees based on some research but mainly on gut feeling. The opinions of others were important references, but I felt wary of the responses.

Upon hearing Pete's and Gary's conflicting views on the same prices, I resolved to know my own mind before seeking opinions in the future. I decided to remain curious, to ask for feedback but always verify before taking it on board. I was fascinated that identical information could receive such different reactions.

Most people do not realize that they have created the world they see. Everything is a reflection of your own ability and mindset:

- Whether prices seem low or high depends on your references.
- Road rage represents your own anger issues, not the careless drivers around you.
- Complaining is blaming others for your reality.
- Frustration is a reflection of failing to demand the best for yourself.

Seeing doom and gloom comes to those who haven't trained themselves to see silver linings. No one can 'make' you feel anything you haven't chosen to feel. Not even Pete or Gary.

I soon realized that Pete's advice was way off. Thinking like Pete and following his guidance would have led to undervaluing myself and my work, scrabbling and competing to win clients who undervalued my work, too. I would have been trapped in a cycle of mediocrity in my aspirations and my contribution, operating well within my ability.

Gary's advice was way off for who I was targeting at the time, but still intriguing. Who were these clients that welcomed higher rates? In the short term I stuck to my prices, but I worked with Gary to meet his clientele and understand their challenges. In the long term I upped my game. I learned more, became more proficient, became confident in front of larger companies, and my prices rose to match.

Most people achieve a tiny fraction of what they are capable of. They settle for less. They get comfortable. They listen to naysayers. They believe uninspiring assertions about their place in the world. They don't question who they are and what they stand for. They don't push themselves beyond their comfort zone. They create excuses for why they haven't achieved more, and they start to believe them.

The 40 per cent rule

Author and extreme athlete David Goggins put his mind and body through insane challenges during the Navy SEAL initiation programme known as Hell Week. The strength and endurance tests include runs, swims and drills, at night and at sea. The challengers carry heavy boats and logs and complete underwater tests. They work in teams with people competing for the same places, all on limited sleep and food. Three out of four people don't complete Hell Week. Their helmets are lined up at graduation as a stark reminder of the courageous attempts that didn't make it.

When Goggins survives another day of Hell Week he's amazed. He keeps asking himself, 'What am I capable of?' Every task he thought he'd fail, every time he was gasping for breath, ready to give up, he dug deeper. He found strength and resilience when he thought they had long run out. 'What am I capable of?' He was capable of much more, and he kept going.

Goggins, writing with Jesse Itzler in his book *Living with a SEAL*, popularized the 40 per cent rule. The 40 per cent rule is simple: when you think you're done, when you cannot give any more, you're only 40 per cent there. You're only 40 per cent of the way to what you're capable of.

If any part of you suspects that you have an incredible gift inside you, if you know your story can resonate, motivate and inspire, if you have ideas and solutions that could change the world, then you owe it to yourself to step up and realize your potential and to see what you are capable of.

Author Hugh MacLeod thinks that 'everybody has their own private Mount Everest they were put on this earth to climb'. Steven Pressfield talks of a shadow life – not the life you could be living if only you would step up, but its shadow. The one far less impressive or exciting. The one that is okay but doesn't make the most of your potential or make you happy.

The realization that you are living a shadow life can hit you like a truck. You're going about your day, convinced of your choices, when you see someone living the life you were afraid to live. There are plenty of healthy-living chefs, but fitness coach, TV presenter and author Joe Wicks put himself out there. There are plenty of people cleaning their own house, but cleaning influencer and author Mrs Hinch dared to dream. For every best-selling book there are thousands of unpublished manuscripts on dusty hard drives, buried under excuses.

Your shadow self might play down someone else's success, calling them lucky, obsessed or privileged. But, inside, you will know that it could have been you.

The 40 per cent rule means remembering you are capable of more. Stepping out of your shadow life requires 100 per cent. Unwavering confidence means deciding what you're going to do and then doing it. Reassessing your plan from the best version of you, not the version influenced by the limitations of others.

My biggest fear is of slipping into a way of thinking and living that does not utilize my full potential. Of accepting something as it is and forgetting how to question the status quo or expect more. Of explaining away what could have been, fitting in and following a safe path. I don't want average or comfort or normality. I want adventure. I want to be remarkable in everything I do. I want to find out how much I am capable of, not live a life of underwhelm.

Do you?

Decide to have an extraordinary ten years. Decide where you'll be by the end of it. Crank the dreaming up a notch or five. Plan how you'll get there. Plan the milestones along the way. Plan the input you will give and the sustained and deliberate effort you will commit to. Make the commitment, persevere with what you suspect will give the most value. Document every step. Make it all happen.

Daily documenting

During 2018 I had a challenging year. I didn't see eye to eye with someone on my team, and our professional relationship was rocky. It had a domino effect on the business, and I spent the year putting out fires that I wasn't sure how had started. My daily fixing of what had gone wrong involved one difficult conversation after another, one difficult decision after another.

Throughout this time I journalled every day. When I look back at the entries, I find fascinating insights into running a business when you feel as if it's running you. But even when things go wrong, you can choose how you respond. In the end it all worked out. The rest of us minimized the disruption and united the team, and the company thrived.

Rereading my entries is like reading a different person's diary. I've grown. I've improved. I am grateful for the challenge because otherwise that growth wouldn't have happened. Not only that, but the journal entries sparked ideas for hundreds of articles that have now helped millions of people. Silver linings will always light the way to remind you what you're capable of. Nothing is insurmountable.

There is little that raises your sense of self-awareness like journalling. Nothing that holds you to account better than writing things down in your diary. Assessing your day. Knowing yourself. Knowing what you want and what you don't want. Picking apart what you did well and where you want to improve. Having a complete sense of who you are and what you're here to do. You look back at challenging times and remember how you smashed through them to where you are now.

Capable of more

Suspecting you're capable of more is a foundation stone in setting up the success you're looking to achieve. Remembering that when you think you're done, you're only 40 per cent there. If you dreamed bigger and pushed harder, what could you be capable of? What could be possible if you hunted success and did not give up? What if you surrounded yourself with people who believed in you and whose minds held no limits? You might surprise yourself.

Decide what you want to achieve and create goals that are so big they scare you. Ask questions of everything that comes your way. Seek regular solitude for uninterrupted and undistracted thought. Document each day and what you learn.

Curiosity is another foundation stone in an extraordinary life and a Ten Year Career. Go on an inquisitive journey of self-awareness. Be intentional in everything you do. Avoid absent-minded decisions and wasting time. See the future of every action you take and where it might lead.

Next, I'll take you through preparing your mind and processes for achieving big in a shorter space of time. Until then, set the foundations. Create a spongey mind ready to absorb the next chapters.

Key takeaways

- Question what others tell you.
- Recognize that you create your own world through ability and mindset.
- Are you stopping at 40 per cent of your capability?
- Journal your way to success.
- Believe that you are capable of more.
- Step out of your shadow self.

Let's find out what you're capable of

Head over to the free *Ten Year Career* companion course for short videos and bonus downloads to apply this chapter's concepts and frameworks to your life and business.
Find it at jodiecook.com/TYC

4

Your Mind Matters

• • •

Humans have approximately 6,200 thoughts per day. Eighty per cent of each day's thoughts tend to be negative and 95 per cent are repetitive: thoughts we've had before.

We are going around like zombies, having almost the exact same thoughts as yesterday.

Thinking in the same way leads to the same results. Your mindset determines not only how you perform but also how you feel about yourself. How you deal with challenges. How you keep going when it's tough. Mindset is your inner compass and the most important tool in your toolbox.

This chapter introduces multiple tools and strategies for levelling up your mind, essential for supercharging your business journey. They include intentional awareness, challenging limiting beliefs, finding inspiration, and understanding your why. We cover bulletproofing your mindset to handle whatever is ahead with ease and grace and remain in the driving seat of your destiny.

If you don't manage your mindset

James was on the warpath, and everyone knew it. He marched around the office looking for prey, leaving destruction in his wake. His communication was via blunt, one-line emails. He assumed the worst before checking, and his reactions governed him.

James projected his stress, uncertainty and pessimism onto his team. They were scared. His dark disposition dictated how his colleagues treated their clients and spoke to each other, how far ahead they planned, and how safe they felt in their role. It led to his company cutting corners, prioritizing reducing costs over adding value. Team members made only the most harmless decisions for fear of retribution. They made decisions only for the short term.

James led the company with his fearful mind, convinced the future would be terrible unless he controlled every element. His mindset wasn't serving him, and his self-awareness was low; everyone around him could feel his fearful aura. James' fondness of the warpath and penchant for wrath created an 'us and them' culture. It led to whispering and gossip. It affected clients.

James' predilection for seeing clients as a nuisance rather than the reason the business existed was neither healthy nor sustainable, and in the end it all fell apart. Team members either didn't stay long or required excessive golden handcuffs to hold on to. Retention and recruitment stifled his business growth.

Fearful leadership might work in a widget factory, where a worker's every action is timed and checked against standards. It doesn't translate to most modern workplaces. A fearful leader managing a distributed team will lose their mind because of their lack of control. Their distrustful demeanour heightens with distance. They consider installing monitoring software and activity sensors. Their team, on the other hand, now free from their physical presence, thrives under freedom or looks for opportunities to rebel. Both outcomes widen the gap between them and the fearful leader.

When you're scared you become a different person. When you're scared you project a future of pessimism. You're led by fear. You tighten up and don't let anyone in. You put up guards to protect what's left. The lizard brain comes in to run the show.

You say things you don't mean and pull others into the fear. You collect evidence of why you're doing the right thing and ignore all the signs that you don't have to do what you're doing. Your behaviour creates a self-fulfilling prophecy that you must control everything, one that cycles for ever. Leading with fear will keep you stuck in the minutiae of your business.

Turning the situation around starts with intentional awareness.

Intentional awareness

'Jodie?' said the driver through the window.

'That's me!' I got in the car.

It was Friday night, and I was taking a taxi home from my best friend's house, a few miles away from mine. This was a regular occurrence, but every journey was different. Some drivers wanted to chat; some asked questions; some told stories. Some played music: trance, pop, classical. Some had the radio on; some listened to podcasts.

They all dropped me at my door, and then I went inside and to sleep. Sometimes I awoke the next morning feeling terrible and not knowing why. I tried to work out the link. It wasn't something I'd eaten or drunk. It wasn't how much sleep I'd had. It was the quality of the sleep. Some nights were restless with crazy dreams; some I slept like a baby.

I realized that how well I slept linked with the taxi driver's choice of entertainment. Chatting, no worries. Music – classical, trance or pop – I slept fine. The news? Terrible.

I started paying attention to my thoughts and feelings on the taxi rides home. When the radio was blaring that day's news stories, even though I wasn't paying much attention, thoughts of pessimism infiltrated my mind. I started worrying about things that I hadn't even known existed two minutes earlier. I had nervous thoughts about all I had to do that weekend or what might happen next week. I wasn't the me I intend to be.

The success you seek relies on making the right decisions from the right mindset. If you aren't intentional, your focus and actions will be misaligned with your true self and higher purpose.

Awareness changed my actions. Now, if a driver has the news on, I ask if they can play music instead. I'm aware of the power of the fear-filled media to change my disposition. My drive home is only a 15-minute journey; what else could make a difference?

When news is in our space it feels real to our lizard brain. When it's playing in our car or being retold by a trusted friend, we feel compelled to listen and respond. In the world of news there's always danger round the corner: hyperinflation, another virus, a decision by some political party. These things very rarely need your attention. The cost is far higher than the attention; it's your mindset.

Whoever thought a late-evening news show was a good idea was mistaken. If I were the prime minister, the first thing I would do would be to ban ten o'clock news bulletins. The wind-down hours before bed are so important to calm and undisturbed sleep. Being well rested during waking hours means better decision making and happier, healthier people.

Keeping up with the news is not essential. It's not urgent in any way. There is nothing anyone needs to know at 10 pm. There are very few real emergencies. Stories of what went wrong and what might happen plant seeds of doubt and spread worry. They keep people thinking small, protecting what they have and believing there isn't enough to go around. Constant reporting, propaganda and commentary instil a mindset of fear. The fear is reinforced by those who also have seen the news and believe that everything is terrible. The fear dictates decisions. The fear controls. The fear perpetuates.

Watch how you feel after scrolling through news stories or social media before bed. After talking about the pandemic, speculating about dangers in the future, gossiping or complaining. Chances are you're irritable, restless and not primed to sleep – as if your energy has been zapped. Even if you think you're exempt, why risk it? Leading or participating in low-energy activities does not inspire happiness, creativity or resourcefulness. Until the nightly news is banned, we can opt out.

Make awareness a game. If 95 per cent of my thoughts are the same as the day before and 80 per cent are negative, I want to find out what they are so I can change them. What are the foods that energize and drain you? The people, the places, the situations, the conversations. What makes you irritable and what makes you visionary? What are the beliefs you hold and accept as truth, even though they might not be?

To understand when something is affecting your mindset, you have to hold a clear definition of the best version of you. When you're at your most happy and relaxed, who are you? How do you feel after reading an inspiring article or having a conversation about great ideas? When you're hanging out with people who bring out the best in you, or when you've quieted your mind's needless chatter and have the clarity of thought and the space to choose well, who are you? This is the version that should show up every single time. The definition should be so strong that you notice if it's changed. You can recognize the shift in energy and pinpoint its cause straight away.

Awareness of your mindset at any given time is paramount. Ask yourself why you are feeling the way you are, pinpoint the cause and trace it back to specific actions or triggers. The next step is making the change. Noticing when fear is leading your thoughts. Noticing when your limiting beliefs are holding you back. Realizing that feelings of insecurity, anxiety or envy are creeping in.

Challenge limiting beliefs

Amanda was considering starting a business. She had been made redundant with a decent pay-out. She wanted to find a way of working from home, seeing her kids more, and having freedom over her time. She needed an idea.

Browsing the internet one day, Amanda took a personality test. It seemed genuine; it was supported by a famous university. Perhaps this would help her find the answers she sought.

Amanda's personality test results showed she had good people skills and worked well in a team. Great. They also told her that she was an executor, not an ideas person. The results suggested she should become the delivery partner to a visionary, but that she was not the visionary type.

Amanda's search for ideas ended right there, and instead she went looking for someone else whose ideas she could deliver. All because of one test, her ambition had changed and her prospects had limited.

Identity is powerful. Humans act consistently with what they believe to be their identity. The person saying, 'I'm going to the gym because I want to lose weight' is far less likely to maintain the practice over time than someone who says, 'I'm going to the gym because I am a person that goes to the gym.' Someone who believes 'I am honest, I am trustworthy, I am reasonable' will have a hard time acting in ways that are incongruent with this identity.

Amanda's identity shifted the day she took that test. It confirmed her fears; she didn't have any good ideas. It gave her the identity of executor and pushed her visionary identity to one side. Because she'd taken a random test on a whim, and not probed any further, this one small action created a self-fulfilling prophecy that limited Amanda's future. Yet one different answer could have given her an entirely different result.

Telling ourselves stories and lines that we believe is like committing tiny acts of sabotage. Stories about our identity, our ability and money can cripple us. It could be someone considering accepting an invitation to deliver a TEDx talk but being told by their mother that everyone in their family gets stage fright and believing that they will, too. Or it could be someone planning to open a new shop being told that it'll never be a success, and then internalizing the sentiment and reconsidering the leap.

48

Limiting beliefs about money are the most damaging because they restrict your future and cause consistent undervaluing of who you are. But we pick them up when we are young and repeat them until we believe they are true. Did you ever hear these phrases used?

- *Money doesn't grow on trees* – instilling the belief that money is scarce and difficult to find.

- *It's too expensive* – creating an association between high price and low value.

- *He's ripping you off* – judging the character of someone selling premium products.

- *She got lucky* – underplaying someone's ability to earn well.

- *Rich people are greedy* – alienating those with money by giving them undesirable qualities.

You can probably think of a friend who talks often about money and the price of things. They look around for discounts and will travel double the time to pay 10 per cent less. They won't buy treats, and they wait anxiously for payday. They are so convinced that money is scarce and their supply limited that they close options for earning. Their belief is limiting their actions.

Perhaps you're that friend.

Life is better when your beliefs serve you. Careers go further when limiting beliefs don't hold you back. When you can focus on having solid values and a healthy relationship with consumption. When you don't need to look at the price of things because you live within your means. When you have confidence in your ability to earn well in return for the value you bring to others.

Flea circuses were popular in the 1800s. Their owners learned a trick to keep their fleas contained. They would put the fleas in a box or jar and add a lid. The fleas, which could jump over eight feet, or 2.4 metres, hit the lid and came back down. They tried one more time; the same happened. Those fleas, which had been jumping over 200 times their height, now only jumped to the height of the container, even when the lid was no longer there.

What are the limiting beliefs putting a lid on your success? Remove the lid's legacy and regain your power.

One day I realized I was operating out of three beliefs:

1. My agency is tying me down.
2. We have to live in Birmingham.
3. My squat is my worst lift.

I wrote them down and unpacked them. The first wasn't true. The team was self-sufficient, my input welcomed but not required. For the previous five years I had spent four months of every 12 living and working in different countries. There was no way the agency was tying me down, but I believed it was, and the belief was stopping me booking more adventures.

I wrote about what was actually happening to reframe the situation in my head and see it in a more helpful way. I wrote that my agency supports my lifestyle. It gives me freedom. I have autonomy over how I spend my time. My team do their jobs well. The team looks after the clients. I am lucky to have a business like this.

I did the same for numbers two and three. Number two linked to number one, and it wasn't true. The exercise helped me see that although Birmingham was where I grew up and had an apartment, its purpose in my life was to be a basecamp. A place from which to travel. The term 'basecamp' was key, and my basecamp could be anywhere.

Belief number three was interesting. I compete in powerlifting, a sport that comprises three lifts. The heaviest you are able to lift for each discipline is known as your one rep max. At the time, my one rep max deadlift was 180 kg (I compete at 57 kg bodyweight). My one rep max bench press was 90 kg. My squat one rep max of 137.5 kg was low compared with the other lifters in my category.

Because of this, I had come to view the squat as my Achilles' heel. It embarrassed me. I would shuffle to the gym on squat days instead of marching with intent, as I did for bench press or deadlift. I never posted squat videos on social media despite doing so with the other lifts, and I resigned myself to believing that the squat might always be my worst lift. When a squat session didn't go so well, I shrugged and told myself it was inevitable.

Without my realizing, my squat belief had formed a narrative around training that affected my actions. Cause and effect had become confused. My belief affected how I acted; I acted like my belief was a fact. I resolved to change it. I went back through previous training logs to see the squat numbers I had hit and the progress I'd seen before.

I started posting squat videos on my Instagram. I made a concerted effort to look forward to each squat training session as much as the others. I told myself that I had all the strength in the world and the perfect proportions for squatting.

Writing down my three biggest limiting beliefs and challenging them was a powerful exercise. Almost instantly I realized that things could be different. I was acting like a flea in a closed container. I was limiting my own jump. I removed the lid, and everything changed.

Practise listening to the limiting beliefs of others. You hear them all the time. What you can and can't do, perhaps on certain days of the week or months of the year. Who will and won't be busy at any given time. What money is and isn't. Other people's generalizations. Methods that don't work anymore cited as the way things are, or untested methods believed unlikely to work.

If you listen to the conversations going on around you, you will hear these acts of sabotage. Collect them up and jot them down. Hear them, recognize them and let them bounce off you. Don't fall for sabotage. Ask, is that true, or do you believe it to be true? Ask it of yourself.

To start, run and complete a career in ten years you need to think differently from nearly everyone else on the planet. You are not a flea. You cannot be limited by ceilings of any kind.

Train yourself to notice limiting beliefs and unhelpful thoughts so as to remove them from your head and vocabulary. Subtract anything in your life that doesn't reflect the best version of you that exists.

How do you break free from limiting beliefs? One way is to unpack them and reassert the opposite. Another is to find role models, examples and reminders that others have succeeded in the way you want to. Or in any way at all.

Finding inspiration

In 2020 I co-wrote a book called *How to Raise Entrepreneurial Kids* with an inspiring person named Daniel Priestley. His work has reached millions of people and has changed their businesses and lives. He is active in sharing his voice to serve his audience of entrepreneurs, and he gives all he can.

When we started writing the book together, I was starstruck. I couldn't believe someone with Daniel's network and reputation had agreed to write a book with me. To be honest, I was a little freaked out.

I had moved far away from inspiration to idolizing, which wasn't helping the book. I was scared that my sections wouldn't be good enough or that my audience wasn't big enough to contribute towards book sales. My attitude gave me writer's block because I felt I had someone to impress; scrappy drafts would not do.

Moving from idolization back to inspiration involved taking a deep breath and recognizing that I was being silly. Daniel was not superhuman. He had reached his level by putting in the work and creating partnerships to open new opportunities, like this one. Magic, genetics, inheritance or trickery hadn't come into it. Once I realized that every aspect of what I admired was accessible, I knew that I could put my feelings of lack aside and focus on writing a great book.

I'm sure you would agree that you see no one as beneath you. You could say with certainty that you treat others as equals and show respect regardless of title or standing.

But what about those you admire? Perhaps you put someone on a pedestal. You see them as incredible or superhuman or something you could never be. You idolize them. It makes little sense to have it both ways. Either there is a hierarchy or there isn't. Far better to believe there isn't. To see astounding greatness as something within your reach.

When I think about who inspires me, they are people who have a mission they want to share. They give generously. They work to deliver their message in accessible ways. They act true to their beliefs. They are humble, kind and patient. They navigate naysayers and are determined about their vision and how they will get there.

Think about the three people who inspire you most and why. Chances are, those qualities we admire in others are those we want to develop in ourselves.

It's easy to idolize but doing so creates a separation between you and someone else and misses the chance to be inspired. It's easy to play down what someone has achieved. It's easy to point to genetics or luck or a head start. There are plenty of people with advantageous genetics, luck or head starts who have done approximately zero with them. There are plenty of people who found a way to succeed from adversity. It's not about what you start with; it's where you end up. It's what you make of the cards you're dealt.

It's easy to be envious. To scroll social media and want what others have. The life, the career, the partner, the house. To wish you had made the choices someone else made and got to where they are now. If you find yourself with feelings of envy, ask yourself if you would want that person's entire life. If the condition was that you could have the part of their life you want only if you exchanged places entirely, would you do it? If you really thought about it, I doubt you would.

There are parts of your life that you would never trade. A straight swap isn't an option. The only option is taking the parts you want to improve and doing so using a cocktail of inspiration and action. Letting yourself be intimidated by someone else doesn't lead anywhere good, only to feelings of lack and low confidence. Be the confident partner, not the adoring fan or envious critic. Don't envy or idolize anyone.

Tap the observer

We make better decisions if we believe not only that someone is watching but that someone is looking out for us. We are more kind, patient and agreeable. We connect with others more easily. For you the observer might be God, the universe, love, a guardian angel or a family member. The semantics aren't important but the concept is; act through the eyes of someone who wants you to do and be your best.

Who inspires you and why? Don't stop at names. Delve into the facet of their personality, life or work that you want to take inspiration from. I don't want to trade places with my friend Daniel, but I admire his quick thinking and way of resonating with everyone he meets. I don't want to trade places with my friend Carrie, but I am inspired by her determination and commitment to showing up to serve her audience. Each person you admire should bring you lessons, not a desire to copy or feelings of envy.

One person I hold in my mind and look up to is future me. My benchmark for growth is past me. It's like current me has a little sister and a big sister. Little sister was naive and excitable, but she was doing the best with that she had at the time. She paved the way for current me. She crossed the ball over for current me to shoot. Big sister is older and wiser and knows more than current me. She's navigating new challenges and she's dreaming bigger. She's using what I set up for her.

Whatever current me chooses to do now is what future me has to deal with. If I skip the gym today, she won't hit the numbers she wants to hit when she competes tomorrow. If I annoy someone today, she has to deal with the repercussions next week. It's my job to set up helpful conditions from which she can thrive.

There is a difference between inspiring and idolizing. One will lift you up and the other will bring you down. The best way of ensuring you can take inspiration while not losing yourself is to know yourself.

Your *why*

Steven Kotler, scientist and author, sees his overriding mission as advancing flow, a concept developed and coined by psychologist Mihaly Csikszentmihalyi. Kotler's work follows this mission. His research, consultancy, courses and books serve to benefit high performers in all fields. The mission gives purpose and meaning to everything he does. Choosing a mission by which he is intrinsically driven means his work feels more like a calling.

Your personal mission statement is your why. It's why you're here. It's what you're here to do. The most effective personal mission statement comprises two parts: how you live and how you serve. Each phase in your life can have a different why, a different purpose. Your why serves as your North Star, your guiding light, the reason you keep going.

- **Personal:** Personal to you. Your version of success. This takes the form 'I will advance', 'I will solve', 'I will inspire', 'I will become'. This puts you as the driver of this mission statement.

- **Mission:** What you're here to do. The backbone of your work and existence. Perhaps you want to discover what you're capable of and help others do the same, as I do. Perhaps you are on a mission to ensure no one is unfairly treated by an employer. Perhaps you want to transform the way we educate kids or stop the oceans filling up with plastic or make your customers feel confident.

- **Statement:** Intentional and definite. In print or on display. Laminated, even. You've thought about it, and it's a commitment. When you have established your mission statement, inspiration without comparison is easy. You can appreciate that others are on their own mission and you are on yours. You no longer see competition. You have acute awareness of what you're here to do.

Airplane security demonstrations instruct that you put on your own oxygen mask before helping another. How you live must come first because you cannot serve others without serving yourself. The world's most generous philanthropists created wealth in abundance first. The world's most incredible peacemakers found their own peace first. Know yourself and be clear how you will live.

The second part is about how you serve. Work out how you and your unique set of skills can most help others. Even if you don't know that, spread good vibes and your calling will become clear. If you do part one well, part two will come to you. It will be clear how you serve, and it might involve being the example that others seek. Setting the bar. Living your own dream and making it okay for them to live theirs. Have your personal mission statement in mind the whole time. Keep focusing on it and see how it brings alignment to your every day.

Figure out, write down and live fiercely by your personal mission statement to align your actions. Without doing work you enjoy, without being genuinely interested in what you're doing, without waking up raring to go, each day will feel like a slog and you won't see your career through. You'll look for escapes, start side projects or succumb to distraction. Great businesses are built on authenticity and sincerity. This path isn't about making a quick buck; it's about a mission that other people buy into as strongly as you. It means work doesn't feel like work.

Perspective

I have been surrounded by troubles all my life long, but there is a curious thing about them – nine-tenths of them never happened.
Andrew Carnegie, industrialist and philanthropist

The education and career conveyor belt we examined in Chapter 1 trained us to think and act in specific ways. To be obedient and accepting. To be so focused on the herd, on news and opinion, that we are susceptible to overreaction. So disconnected from others that we see only heroes or villains, lovers or enemies. Gullible to a clickbait head-line and liable to go down a rabbit hole of doom scrolling or a spiral of fearful thoughts.

Being able to find perspective is paramount.

Business leader and *New York Times* best-selling author Michael Singer found a way to gain and keep perspective. When he discovered meditation, he found inner calm. It meant he reconsidered everything in his life from a new perspective, and it changed him. He credits his daily meditation practice with ensuring he is always in the best mind-set. He found many choices easier to make. He found calmness more easily, and he found that people gravitated towards him.

If I'm feeling low, it's because I've lost a sense of perspective. I'm mistaking a danger or worry that's in my thoughts for one that is clear and present. That worry is all I can think about and I'm convinced everyone else is thinking about it, too. It clouds my judgement and obscures my vision. I am projecting my fear onto my future reality, so I'm feeling low and uninspired.

Make a pact with yourself to not be tricked into thinking a per-ceived danger is bigger than it is. Apply the clear and present rule. If there's a grizzly bear standing right in front of me, that's a danger that's clear and present. Not much else fits the bill. Is the danger I am worried about clear and present? Usually, the answer is no. It likely will not matter in five years, or even one year. So why worry now?

One CEO I know uses the analogy of a helicopter to find perspec-tive. When she notices she is too far in the detail she boards a meta-phorical helicopter to see her organization with some distance. She keeps a small toy helicopter on her desk as a reminder. She also thinks about great leaders who have gone before her and finds comfort in knowing that they went through similar situations.

Memento mori is a Latin phrase that means 'Remember you will die'. *Memento mori* appears on T-shirts and in Twitter bios. I've seen it on laptop stickers. Every time you open your laptop, remember you will die. Keeping mortality at the forefront of their mind is all the per-spective some people need to shift from an unproductive to a construc-tive mindset. For a similar reason, I like walking around cemeteries. I see rows of gravestones from people who walked the earth, saw their friends and did their work, like me. One day you won't be here, and neither will anyone you know. So what really matters?

How do you find and maintain perspective? Perhaps you have an analogy, a mantra or an exercise. Find something that resonates with you and use it whenever you need to. Make perspective your superpower. You're going to need it.

The best version of you

The best version of me is smiling. She's feeling zen. She glides through the day with ease and grace and looks forward to every interaction. She sees others through the eyes of love and compassion. She is at peace. She's content in the present and feels grateful for everything in her life.

To recognize and make a change when you're at your worst, become familiar with what you're like at your best. Know when the best version of you is present so you may find them more often.

The best version of me can exist in any situation. She's not weather-dependent; she isn't affected by the day's headlines or anything that may be happening at work. This version can be present when work is piling up, when I'm tired or hungry, or I'm at a busy airport.

How would you describe the best version of you? How do they feel and act? What do they say? Define you at your best. When you're in your element. When you feel true to who you are and at your most peaceful. Write it down. Internalize it as an objective, a compass. Consistently bringing your best self to every situation will become a habit.

Your best self is the one who has great ideas, executes well and can amass a tribe. The more known they are to you, the more you can summon them when they go awry.

Lizard taming list

Operating from your lizard brain will never represent the best version of you. It's responsible for all the worst parts of anyone's personality. The scarcity, the fear, the fight-or-flight behaviours, the anger. The unsympathetic you. Those comments made with disdain or a touch of ridicule? Those are the lizard brain talking.

Combat the lizard brain by making a lizard taming list. When you notice you're anything other than the best version of you, have tools ready so you can switch states as soon as possible. The purpose of the

list is to make interventions that bring perspective and reclaim the optimal you, rather than falling into escapism or mind-numbing activities
to make you forget who you are.

When I'm feeling rubbish, I turn to my lizard taming list and do
something on it. I go for a walk, call an energizing friend, eat some
vegetables, or breathe more deeply and consciously. I subscribe to the
Calm app, so I do the 'Daily Calm', a ten-minute meditation on a different theme. I answer Calm's question 'How are you feeling?' to track
moods over different days. I recite the mantras that help banish unhelpful thoughts. One of these is 'I am the hero of my own life', the title
of a guided journal by Brianna Wiest. Hearing it jolts me into taking
control of my mind and actions. Another is: 'I can and I will; watch me.'

I once picked up a leaflet from the UK National Lottery about a
game called Set For Life. The top prize of this lottery was £10,000 per
month for 30 years. My company had hit this milestone soon after its
inception, yet I always felt pressure to earn more. The pressure was
self-inflicted. I was comparing myself to others, to people I admired,
and feeling inferior. I pinned the leaflet up for a regular reminder to
switch my mindset to grateful. I was set for life and had already won
the Lottery. With this newfound perspective and money worries out of
the way, I could relax and focus on more productive thoughts.

Objects to help you switch your mindset could include a picture
of someone you love, a thank-you letter you received, or an award you
won. Pin them to the walls and your desktop or phone background as
regular reminders.

Define your objects, mantras or interventions and put them within
easy reach, to switch your mindset when required. Move from lizard to
visionary to bring the best version of you.

A questioning mindset

I once booked a trip to Amsterdam. I mentioned it to a friend who had
been there before. 'Oh,' she said, 'you have to get a bike while you're
there. You absolutely must. It's the only way to do Amsterdam right.'
I thought, why? It's easy to hear an opinion and feel like you have an
obligation. In reality, you can do whatever you want. There are plenty
of ways to explore Amsterdam.

The quality of your life depends on the quality of your questioning. People who don't ask enough questions experience slow-moving careers and suboptimal mindsets. Growth requires seeking answers and not accepting anything at face value. Dreaming big requires comparing what is with what could be. Optimum mindsets require conscious and deliberate interventions.

During my graduate scheme, when I was training to be a leader, we spent two days every two months in specific leadership training. On day one we split into small groups and took turns outlining a challenge from our placement. The rule was that you could ask questions only of the person in the spotlight. Simple questions. Leading questions weren't allowed, and neither was giving options. The questions had to come from curiosity rather than superiority. You couldn't mask advice as a question. The team member in the spotlight answered the questions until they figured something out.

The group coaching not only taught us how to ask better questions to help someone find solutions, it also taught us to handle interrogation without getting defensive. There were times long after my graduate scheme was over that I imagined myself in that group coaching environment. I thought hard about what questions my teammates might have asked and how to answer them.

You can replicate this process to similar effect. Think of a friend who asks good questions. Ask them if they can ask you question after question about your specific challenge. Lay out the rules in advance – that you're not looking for advice or steering. Say you're experimenting with the way forward and you value their questions as part of that.

The more advanced stage is doing this with yourself. When you don't require that friend, when you can find and ask yourself questions that lead you to epiphanies and progress, is when your questioning mindset is firmly established.

If questions aren't asked, no answers come forward, and everything stays the same. Not questioning leads to the same thoughts, arguments, habits and frustrations. The same comfort zone and discomfort zone parameters. Doing the same things will yield the same results. But we want better results.

In Chapter 1 I asked you to question outdated beliefs and the way you are being led unconsciously. Questioning is one of the best tools to use throughout your Ten Year Career journey. Questioning more means accepting less at face value. It means hearing sentence starters such as 'You have to...' and 'It's always...' and sensing alarm bells. What do you mean I have to? I don't have to do anything! Tell a kid they have to put their coat on and it's clear that they have no problem questioning what adults accept. What about you?

As kids we ask questions all the time, often to the point of annoying adults. Sometimes kids ask the questions that everyone is thinking and the adults who don't want to answer mumble something and change the subject. As adults we question far less. We think we know the answers.

The truth is, we do know a lot of the answers. Questioning not only brings out the answers we are hiding, deep down in our subconscious, it also highlights gaps in our knowledge and understanding that we can fill.

Ask yourself

My book *Stop Acting Like You're Going to Live Forever* has an accompanying guided journal. It's a book of questions. The guided journal is designed to increase self-awareness and understanding by asking the questions that a reader might not ordinarily ask themselves. The power of questions to spark realizations or change someone's thinking is huge.

When questioning, everything is up for grabs. You could ask yourself one question that changes everything.

When you don't know what to do, ask questions. When you're feeling unsure, ask questions. When you're taking a big step, ask questions. Revisit your assumptions to check if they still hold true. When you want to make a change, ask questions. How do I want to feel? How could I feel great now? If I knew what to do, what would I do?

Every answer has a question that retrieves it. When I started out in business, my question was, 'How can I retire by the time I'm thirty?' A tech company CEO might ask, 'How can my app warrant a £100 million exit?' The owner of a chain of coffee shops might ask, 'How can we open 20 new shops this year?' Any business owner could ask, 'How can we double in size?' 'How can we find more of our perfect customers?' 'What can we do this week to get closer to our goals?'

As you're reading this book, ask yourself similar questions. How can I not need to work within ten years? How can I take what I'm doing to the next level, and the one after that? How can I zoom out and make audacious plans? What do I need to do to make my dream a reality? If I didn't need to work, what would I do? What would the best version of me do next? What are my unique strengths in making this happen? If not now, when?

Asking bigger questions forces your brain to scramble to answer them. It also forces perspective and keeps distractions and the lizard brain at bay. When I was thinking about how to find a sponsor for 24,000 sets of storybooks, smaller worries just disappeared. When you're working out how to sell your business, you care less about football scores. Leaders of the world's biggest companies are solving huge problems, not sending emails about Secret Santa. Entrepreneurs on a mission are putting the work in, not sitting around in groups gossiping. Bigger, better questions. Bigger, better solutions.

Being able to change your mindset immediately leads to improvement across the board. Find one method of keeping perspective that means you're in a productive state for more of your day. You could change one thing that means your life is unrecognizable in ten years or even ten days. When you've mastered changing your mindset, work on strengthening your mind.

How to strengthen your mind

'Oh no, not another one.'

When I was a student at the University of Sheffield, I joined the cross-country team. Our training for cross-country races, 10 km races and half marathons involved a mix of short and long runs, track drills, fartlek (mixed-speed drill) training and hill sprints. Sheffield is a very hilly city. The whole team hated hill training and especially hated it when it was raining. Dragging yourself out of your cosy student house to run up hills in the pouring rain is no one's idea of fun, and it definitely wasn't mine.

I hated hills with a passion. I hated the out-of-breath feeling at the top, how the incline made my quads feel, how much hills threw my running times out because I had to go so slowly. I hated feeling as though I was going to faint. I hated all the smug runners who overtook me on the way up.

Yet there in front of me, for the fifth time that day, was another steep hill.

The cross-country coach didn't care if it was cold, or raining, or hilly. When we were hill training, he would have the whole team chant 'We love the hills' as we ran up them. When it was raining, he had the whole team chant 'We love the rain'. We'd chant it over and over, for the entire training session. We were being subliminally conditioned to commit to training regardless of external circumstances. The coach taught us not only how to inhabit the space beyond our comfort zone but how to grow to love it.

Everyone has a comfort zone. Inside your comfort zone is everything that keeps you the same. That stable role, that dead-cert opportunity, the dream house and its soft furnishings. That level of responsibility that's exactly right. Those questions you could answer in your sleep.

The perimeter of each individual's comfort zone differs. You might have no problem turning up to an event alone, giving a live interview, or making Christmas dinner for 12. Deadlines or confrontation or sky-diving might not faze you. But you may be very nervous around horses. Or flying. Or at a karaoke bar.

Outside your comfort zone is everything that makes you stronger. Outside your comfort zone lie new experiences, new people and new opportunities. It's everything that means you are better placed for dealing with any future. The definition of settling is staying within your comfort zone. Even someone who can present on camera, take part in extreme sports and perform for huge crowds might be stagnant; their comfort zone is just bigger.

I sold my agency to expand my comfort zone. Although running a team, looking after clients and experiencing agency life might not be everyone's idea of fun, it was mine. I loved it so much that I welcomed every challenge, but I started to see the same challenges. The new challenge became teaching my team to navigate them. They did brilliantly. Their comfort zones expanded. Mine stayed the same. I didn't see myself as someone who would run the same business for decades.

I wanted bigger problems. The future was unknown, but I was ready to go after it.

Not everyone moves towards those feelings. Most people stay in their comfort zone.

Beyond the comfort zone is the discomfort zone. This is where you feel overwhelmed and out of your depth, as if you want the world to open up and swallow you whole. It's where your heart rate increases and you feel anxious and trip over your words.

The strongest people in the world, in mind and body, push past their comfort zone and seek their discomfort zone. They are hellbent on growth, and they want to see what they are capable of. They know that reaching their discomfort zone will expand their comfort zone so much that it's unrecognizable to their former self.

Strengthening your mind and being able to handle anything that comes your way involves expanding both your comfort and discomfort zones. Whatever makes you nervous, that's what you need to do. Whatever gives you butterflies holds the biggest opportunity for growth.

The zone of the unknown

Most aspects of the future are unknown. I don't know what will happen tomorrow. I don't know how someone will respond to some work I put out there. I don't know what will happen if I ask a question or try something new or what might be on the news. I can plan ahead as best as possible, but things change, people move on and the unexpected occurs.

The zone of the unknown refers to anything that lies ahead that isn't defined or planned. It's anything subject to change by external circumstances, which is pretty much everything.

It's human nature to choose familiar discomfort over the unknown possibilities of joy. This explains why people stay in jobs they don't enjoy and avoid taking risks. It's why they visit the same restaurants or holiday destinations year upon year. It's summed up in proverbs like 'A bird in the hand is worth two in the bush', 'Better the devil you know' or 'Keep your enemies closer'.

Actually, the two birds in the bush could offer a far juicier prospect than the one in the hand. The proverbial devil is taking the place of those angels you might find if you were only looking for them. Keeping your enemies close means putting up with their bullshit. Not one of those scenarios is optimizing for the future, but each represents safety. In each proverb, the danger feels managed and we hold on to the security of the known.

I'm training myself to love the zone of the unknown in the same way I grew to love hills.

Consider the opposite. Imagine you never reached your comfort zone's edges, felt your heart skip a beat or felt that rush of adrenalin. You might think that sounds awesome, that it would mean you felt relaxed and calm every day. The reality is that your comfort zone would shrink and smaller obstacles would appear bigger. A concept known as mushrooming says that in the absence of big problems, small ones grow disproportionately large. Feeling out of your depth, therefore, as well as unsure, nervous or out of control, can only be a good thing. Each encounter leads to growth. Discomfort means progress.

If I can associate feelings of discomfort with inevitable positive outcomes, I can train my first reaction to change to be one of optimism. I can remember that there are rarely breakdowns, only breakthroughs. By being okay with forgoing the safe option in favour of what could be, and understanding that everything I'm looking for is on the other side of fear, I remember that the future, while uncertain, carries opportunity.

Throughout your Ten Year Career journey there will be discomfort. Welcome it. Where it would be easy to cancel, postpone or choose the easy thing, the results you seek require moving through discomfort and creating a new comfort zone. I have found that, paradoxically, choosing to do the easy things leads to a hard life, and choosing to do the hard things leads to an easy life – a life where work is a choice and every day feels like a Saturday.

Seeking to overcome the eye-watering discomfort found within the zone of the unknown equips you to be superhuman in response to anything less. It leaves you convinced you can handle anything that is thrown at you.

Resilience

We suffer more from imagination than reality.

Seneca, ancient Roman philosopher

Harriet missed a call. She missed a call from an important client who normally wouldn't have called her. She saw the name on the screen and panicked. Her lizard brain sprang into action and it freaked out. What could he want? We only spoke a few days ago. What could he possibly need to ask me? She started to worry. What if he was calling to say he wasn't happy or that he wanted to leave?

She thought about it for an hour or so, struggling to concentrate on other work because the missed call was in the back of her mind. At some point she decided enough was enough. She took a deep breath and called back.

'Oh, hi, Harriet,' a friendly voice said. 'I wondered if you could tell me the name of the proposal software you use. We love it, and we want to start using it for ours.'

Even something perceived as difficult could end up being fine or easy, but unless it's addressed head on we'll never know what we're capable of. Overcoming any adversity, however trivial, is another check in the 'I can handle this' box.

Every business is better run by a resilient leader. One who stays calm and collected and responds rather than reacts. The hot-headed boss who stomps around is likely not in control of how they are acting. Neither is the salesperson who blurts out the wrong words, the writer who can't focus, or the start-up owner struggling to remember their pitch.

The ability to bounce back after tough times is resilience. It's a measure of elasticity. Of how quickly you can spring into an optimum position and mindset. It's how well you can return to the best version of you.

Not practising resilience until tough times crop up is a passive strategy of self-improvement. A better plan is seeking out the tough things and doing them every day. It means heading straight for the situations and conversations that others might shy away from.

Ben Horowitz's book *The Hard Thing about Hard Things* differentiates hard things from easy things. The easy things are the ones everyone loves. Giving good news, making audacious plans and hiring great people. Easy-peasy. The hard things are giving bad news, falling short of your milestones and firing people who aren't that great. It's in the hard things that resilience builds.

The right thing to do is often the hardest. The one most avoided. The one that's put off to next week or deemed too tricky to tackle head-on. But it's the thing that's the most important by a long way.

Willpower is at its highest in the morning and runs out throughout the day, like a video game character whose energy bar shortens as they run and jump. Tackling the hardest thing first is one way of making the most of the peaks and troughs of willpower. Another is putting your mind and body through a series of willpower challenges to reaffirm how resilient you are.

One source of building resilience is physical. Wim Hof is an extreme athlete from the Netherlands, famous for withstanding freezing temperatures for extended periods. The Wim Hof Method, taught to entrepreneurs and athletes alike, combines breathing techniques and cold exposure, with benefits including improved cognitive function and stress reduction. One element of the Wim Hof Method is cold showers. In Hof's own words, 'A cold shower a day keeps the doctor away!' The method recommends first adding 15–30 seconds of cold at the end of your normal shower, before progressing to an entire cold shower. Soon you will be able to sit happily in a bath of icy water. Fans of the Wim Hof Method include prominent figures Tim Ferriss, Joe Rogan and Ross Edgley. Exposure to the cold can reduce someone's resting heart rate, leading them to feel refreshed and better able to withstand the rollercoaster of entrepreneurship.

I hate the idea of being cold. At first it was a big step to turn the shower handle from toasty to chilly. But when I'm standing there in the freezing cold, breathing through it, I feel invincible. I go from tolerating the temperature to enjoying it. The cold water is a metaphor for running a business. The journey is going to be relentless. Whatever is thrown at you will feel as though it's on a mission to bring you down. It will come at you and keep going, and your only recourse is how you manage your mind to deal with and even enjoy it.

Solving the right problem

Andrew runs a team of developers. Together they create websites and complex web applications. Andrew had a problem. His team built beautiful apps that appeared to work well, but they would always break once the customer had them. He puzzled over what was happening and why it kept happening.

The developer was creating and testing each app the way a customer should use it. He was testing every button they would click and the options they might choose and following the payment process they would follow. To him, all worked fine. The app was speedy, looked great and got a customer from A to B. What was the problem?

The problem is that customers don't go from A to B. They go via D, J, M and Z. The developer thought someone would travel a linear journey through the app, forgetting that those using it are complex beings with other factors at play.

Someone might be making a purchase using the app when the doorbell rings and they go to answer it. When they return, the screen has frozen because there's no time-out mechanism. They might put items in their cart, only to go back a step to check another thing they wanted to buy. They might select one colour option only to change their mind. They might send the screen to a friend halfway through. They might have misplaced their credit card, have questions about a certain step or use the app in another way than the logical one the developer envisaged.

Andrew discovered it was a testing problem. The existing testing process used linear thinking. The problem was the team was not testing non-standard app usage. The problem was assuming that users would take only logical steps. Creating a checklist for testing didn't change the outcome, and customers were still disappointed. Instead, Andrew made the goal of testing very simple: break the app.

Once the goal shifted from *test the app is working* to *break the app*, testing became a game that everyone loved to play. The developer who made the app thought more about how the app could be broken and put mechanisms in place just in case. The testers were determined to use the app in the craziest ways possible to break it. The motivation behind the process had changed. That meant the app performed better, with fewer bugs and crashes.

The human brain represents only 2 per cent of a human's mass, yet it uses about 20 per cent of the energy. Expending precious brainpower on solving the wrong problems is a complete waste. The energy has to come from somewhere else, representing inefficiency.

You might be working on problems that simply aren't the right ones to solve. For anything that crops up, if you keep going back a step, you eventually find the root cause. Finding the root cause means you can solve the actual problem and get back on track with your progress. Everything else is a mask, or a short-term workaround that misses the point.

Your problem isn't what a team member said to a customer. The problem is that they didn't know it wasn't appropriate – it's a training problem. Or is it a hiring problem? Could it be a rushing problem? You're onboarding clients with a frequency that requires hiring fast, and there isn't a chance to train new recruits properly. Sounds like a vision problem. Or a pricing problem. Perhaps you're too cheap. You're racing to the bottom, and the only way to keep up is by cutting quality.

What's the true problem you are solving? At his third Olympic Games, having lost in nearly all his previous races, rower Ben Hunt-Davis won Olympic gold at the Sydney Olympics in 2000. His subsequent book, with the title *Will It Make the Boat Go Faster?*, is a sterling example of solving the right problem. In the case of Hunt-Davis, details were irrelevant if they didn't contribute to making the boat go faster. Outfit choices, press, daily activities – each had to contribute.

Always connect what you are doing to why you are doing it. Hunt-Davis wanted to win a gold medal. He was solving a speed problem. When I was a teenager, I worked incredibly hard at being a waitress because I was seeking independence. I wanted to earn enough to take driving lessons and buy myself a car. It was in the back of my mind for every shift: my own car, so I could go anywhere I wanted. I was solving a mobility problem.

When striving towards a big exit, a smooth-running business or an extraordinary life, expending your energy in the right way is paramount and what keeps you focused. What is the overriding problem you're trying to solve or question you're striving to answer, and why does it matter?

Philosopher and psychologist John Dewey observed that 'a problem well put is half-solved'. Persistently define the problem you are solving to avoid wasting brainpower solving peripheral problems or applying fixes that don't stand up to testing.

Resourcefulness

Babies are resourceful. When they are hungry or tired or need a nappy changed, they will make sure everyone knows. They will not settle until their needs are met. Children are resourceful. They will open drawers and cupboards and create games out of everyday objects. They will grasp concepts that adults overlook. They will ask questions when they don't know, rather than assume a sub-context. They are open to learning and do not discount solutions before trying them.

Addicts are resourceful. Anyone addicted to their phone will know the effort they will make to find a charger when it's out of battery. Or steer the conversation towards a topic that requires getting it out of their pocket. Addiction to drugs or alcohol is no different; the lengths taken for a fix can be extraordinary. Imagine if that resourcefulness was channelled into saving the planet or making discoveries that changed lives.

The ability to assemble resources and amass support is paramount to a Ten Year Career. The audacity to act depends on how much you want it. On your journey, be like the baby or the addict. Work out what you need and how to get it. Knock on new doors. Try the windows. Tunnel in if you need to.

Everyone is born resourceful. They either keep and develop the trait or they learn how to be helpless. Listen for learned helplessness. You'll hear it from that person who believes there's just no use in trying because it didn't work last time, or there's no point asking because last time the answer was no. They might complain that there's no use starting that sport or business because an injury may flare up again or the market just isn't right. Learned helplessness means assuming a situation is hopeless, and that is the reason not to start.

As we go through life and work picking up rejections, failures and hearing no, our confidence can be gradually chipped away. The most resourceful among us see past the stumbles. We find another way, try a different angle or ask someone else. We look into the future, think about what might happen next and create solutions for the way forward. The solution may not be found straight away – it might take a while before it comes to light – but a resourceful person will uncover every option.

Most roles and their associated work can be done in a resourceful way and an unresourceful way. Unresourceful means plodding along, doing things slowly, waiting for opportunities to arise instead of going after them. It does not lead to making a bigger mark in a shorter space of time.

Resourceful people who are clear on their why will always find a way to figure something out, often with spectacular results. They get a reputation for being resourceful and more seems to come their way.

Confidence

My social media agency had a meeting pod in the office. It was an elegant, curved glass contraption we invited visitors into. They would always comment. They named it the 'glass case of emotion' (a reference to the film *Anchorman*), 'the confession box' and sometimes 'the office shower', because of the way the door slid across to close.

The pod heard some stories, that's for sure. We met people who came for help with their marketing. Over a coffee in the pod, they told us about their business or business idea, convinced that it was going to change the world. They believed the problem they solved was colossal and that they were the hero to bring the solution to every sufferer.

It would have been easy for us to roll our eyes and chalk their enthusiasm down to naivety, to dismiss them as another buffoon with an unrealistic dream. We never did. In fact, the enthusiasm was infectious. Confidence is enthralling. Confidence is attractive. It meant my team got caught up with their vision and started thinking of ideas for how we could get their message out there. The visitor would leave and we'd carry on talking about the campaigns we could run and the work we could do for them.

It's inspiring to see someone's huge confidence in their idea and ability and see them convinced that they will make it happen. Many did. Many were right, and my team helped them get there. If someone is truly determined, they will channel their confidence into action and find a way.

Plenty of feats once considered impossible were achieved by those who dared to dream. There was no reason that the people who visited our meeting pod with their ideas couldn't make them happen. If the problem exists, sooner or later someone will solve it. Why couldn't it be them?

If you visited my team in the meeting pod, would you have been the same? Would we have felt your enthusiasm for your business, your passion for your plans, and felt confident that you would execute as needed? Would we have believed in you because it was abundantly clear that you believed in yourself? Would we have felt excited to work with you, to join forces and spread your message far and wide?

One question I love is, 'What do I know for sure?' Those people in the meeting pod had a dream, an idea and inclination to make something happen. The change they wanted to make had an audience, however small. I knew for sure it was possible. I didn't know for sure they would make the right decisions or put the required work in. I didn't know if we could help make their business a success. For each conversation we focused on what we knew for sure, so we could be the supportive and enthusiastic partner they sought.

When you choose to be inspired rather than sceptical, magic happens. Your brain thinks in a way more conducive to success. Your energy makes people want to be around you. Masking cynicism as realism, or playing devil's advocate, is rarely a good look. No one is looking for someone else to dampen their spark, and if someone consistently dampened yours, you would stop telling them things.

What many don't realize is that the confidence you have in other people is proportionate to the confidence you have in yourself. When you have unwavering belief in your own capability (not arrogance, confidence), when you realize you have defied countless odds being alive today and you know you will figure anything out, you are believable. If you find yourself dismissing the plans of others and belittling their ideas, it's a sign of doubt in yourself.

Extreme athlete and ex-Navy SEAL David Goggins, whom we met in Chapter 3, has a technique for building a bank of confidence ready to dip into whenever he needs it. He calls it 'the cookie jar'. Your personal cookie jar is a list of reminders of all those things you thought you would never get over and then did. Of those things you achieved despite adversity. All the mountains you thought you'd never summit. Those times you weren't sure what would happen and then you smashed it. The cookie jar exists so that you can dip into the examples and regain the confidence that went awry. It's a journal entry to revisit, time and time again, until the confidence comes naturally.

Psychologist Rick Hanson said your brain is like Velcro for the negative but Teflon for the positive. Remembering the reasons why you can't is easy but remembering the reasons why you can takes work.

When you hit those inevitable bumps in the road, or you're having a bad day and have doubts about your path, how will you regain confidence? Big plans, such as not needing to work within ten years, require audacity.

No one tentatively broke a world record, cautiously delivered a powerful speech or gingerly landed on the Moon. No one warily won a life-changing contract or conservatively sold a million products.

Confidence, fearlessness even, is essential to everything you're looking to achieve.

Confidence means knowing for sure that you're onto something and being ready for the journey. You are unflustered and unfazed and welcome a challenge. Deep down, you are convinced you're heading in the right direction with your business or your way of doing things. Cool, calm and collected. Confidence is impressive and infectious. It overcomes objections, ensures you start and finish strong, and is a key tool in your toolbox.

Implement these mindset tools to ensure your mind is always on your side. It matters. Next, we'll get you unequivocally set up for success, no matter which stage of your business you are in.

Key takeaways

Use these skills to manage your mindset away from fear:
- Become intentionally aware of what affects your mindset.
- Become aware of your limiting beliefs.
- Find inspiration.
- Understand and articulate your why.

Use these skills to strengthen your mindset:
- Pull back to seek the right perspective.
- Embody the best version of you.
- Defend yourself with a lizard taming list.
- Develop a questioning mindset.
- Expand your comfort zone.
- Do the hardest things first.
- Cultivate resourcefulness.
- Exude confidence.

Put all of this together to change the way you think.

Master your mind

Head over to the free *Ten Year Career* companion course for short videos and bonus downloads to apply this chapter's concepts and frameworks to your life and business.
Find it at jodiecook.com/TYC

5

Set Up For Success

• • •

By mid-December of 2014 I was frazzled. Having spent the year being everywhere, I couldn't wait for a break. I craved Christmas and some space to think and breathe. I was going to morning, lunch and evening networking events and speaking on stage at half of them. I won a business award that led to a flurry of invitations hitting my inbox. Every week I was on the train to London and other cities, to run courses for new and returning clients. I was going to sales meetings all over the country and had a team working on account management for a growing list of brands.

My to-do list was never finished: there were always new entries. My team was progressing. They became knowledgeable and resourceful and knew when to ask for help. It was chaos of the most magical kind, but it was completely unsustainable.

I spent the year saying yes to every invitation, with the goal of seeing what was possible. Seeing who I could meet and what I could learn. Where it would lead. It led to rushing around being busier than ever, but with loads of silver linings. I loved handling this level of work intensity for a year, but it was time to work out a better system. I needed to stop spinning so many plates lest one dropped.

As soon as January arrived, I worked out how to set myself up for success and stay there. In this chapter I'll show you what I learned. We introduce the Ten Year Career framework and cover what is required of you in each phase. They are:

1. Execute

2. Systemize

3. Scrutinize

4. Exit

I'll also show you how to define the playing field before determining who you are and what you want. I cover the power of intention, making your mark, starting as you mean to go on, and the crucial element of knowing the endgame.

Phases of entrepreneurship

Every business is different. Every stage of every business is different. Starting up, scaling up, doing more or less, looking to exit – each commands a different approach.

Entrepreneurs often confuse their stages. A friend setting up a skiwear ecommerce store had a typical experience. His orders had shown a promising start, but he didn't know how to grow them. He watched a law of attraction video and considered – and these were his actual words – 'sitting back and letting the money flow'. But the universe – however it does work – doesn't work like that.

At the other end of the spectrum are business owners who do questionable things at questionable times – CEOs of huge companies who don't trust their people meddle in every decision or focus on the detail to the detriment of the bigger picture. They think too small, when what their team needs them to do is make big plans and steer the ship, not run the giftshop.

A good leader engages in an optimal set of actions at each stage. The same actions can mark tremendous catastrophe or roaring success depending on timing. With the goal of work being a choice, the building blocks must be laid in the right order. Going back a step creates confusion for you and your team and unsettles the foundations you carefully laid.

At the start, your business is all about, well, starting up. Saying yes, having conversations, testing hypotheses, and moving fast to run experiments and make edits. You work to establish a market, a customer base or a unique selling point and become known. This is the time to go all-hands-on-deck and put all irons in the fire. Learn by doing, not by overthinking.

During this stage you are busy. You are busy building a company, a product, a network or a dossier of feedback. This is where my skiwear entrepreneur friend should have been hanging out, laying the groundwork, turning over every stone and growing a customer base.

On the flipside, although some businesses might appear to be mature, many are still in the execute phase because they don't have systems and processes, or because the owner is overly involved in the everyday.

This is why, as the leader of a solid business, your focus has to be systemizing (that's what I had to get to after December 2014). I knew I had reached this stage because my workload had become unsustainable. I was needed in more than one place at once. The agency was growing quickly, and my competent teammates were ready to take on more. While mine was a good problem to have, it required a different approach.

During systemize you take what you learn from the execute phase and make a series of decisions. What do we continue with? (This should now be obvious.) What do we drop completely? (Also obvious.) What do we automate and delegate? What should you be doing? What should I be doing? How do we want the next five years to look and how do we take what we know and make a plan for that to happen?

In order to progress to phase three, your execution should be world class and your systems stand up to questioning. What matters now is scrutinizing. The business should be running like a well-oiled machine and, all being well, you should be getting bored. This is where you decide what you want, which might be to prepare for an exit, run a lifestyle business, or re-enter the execute phase in a new way. Darren, the new owner of my social media agency, had reached the scrutinize stage when we met. Running agencies is his jam. He loves working with his team, he loves his clients, he loves every part of his work. He wanted to see where he could take this collective ability. Darren scrutinized. He zoomed out and spoke to big thinkers, removed limiting beliefs, and made big plans about the superagency he wanted to create. The superagency in Darren's mind came to fruition as he acquired agencies that met his standards.

That December of 2014 I graduated from the execute phase and was ready to systemize. Until then I hadn't thought about it. In 2011, if you had asked me what my business plan was, I would have laughed and told you it was two words: get clients. If you had asked me about my systems, my goals and visualization practice, I would have told you I didn't have time because I was too busy establishing my company.

I could tell you that I planned every stage of my Ten Year Career. That the execution stage was intentional; I was meeting as many people as I could, speaking at as many events as possible and learning every role within my agency by doing it myself, so that when I hired people to deliver each one the benchmark would be set. I would tell you that saying yes to every invitation and working out the logistics after was part of a masterplan to reach the next stage with the most data possible.

In reality, that wasn't the case. I was naively going for it without a second's thought of anything else. I wasn't thinking about the future of the business or my ten-year goals. It was simply about meeting people, signing clients and doing great work for them.

Hindsight is a wonderful thing, but it doesn't blind me to the fact that I didn't know a lot, and in particular I didn't know what I didn't know. When I was in the execute phase, I didn't know there were other distinct stages of running a business beyond executing well. Being mindful back then of the other phases in my Ten Year Career would have served me well. Nevertheless, the execute phase, with its curiosity and busyness, had a purpose. Without the insights that come from intense execution, I would be guessing about what I had to delegate and how, and about what to do next.

Knowing the phases and which you are in, coupled with the corresponding focus, gives purpose and intention to action. It means having processes in mind throughout the execute phase, but with your strategy being to test, learn and say yes. It means doing some scrutinizing from the start, but so you bring your best self to every endeavour, not that you're so zoomed out that you miss the details.

Visualization

In an experiment conducted by psychologist Judd Biasiotto at the University of Chicago showing the effectiveness of visualization on free throws, he split basketball players into three groups. The first group practised free throws every day for an hour. The second group visualized making free throws but didn't practise. The third group did nothing. The result? Group one (practice) and group two (visualization) improved by 24 per cent and 23 per cent, respectively. Group three made no improvement.

When Andre Agassi won Wimbledon in 1992, he said it felt like déjà vu because he had already won it in his mind, but he still had to deliver on the court. In something you are already proficient in, like the basketballers and their freethrows, visualization alone might work out. For everything else, including business, it's not a shortcut for missing practice or putting the miles in. Visualization is not a substitute for hard work. You can't just 'sit back and let the money flow'.

During my execution phase I visualized in a vague way. I knew I wanted to win clients and I had half an idea of the type of clients I would love to work with. I had ideas about what my first office might look like and the types of personalities my first team members might have.

The mental pictures ramped up for the systemize phase. I pictured my business as a smooth-running machine, in which everyone knew what they were doing and why. I pictured winning clients without having spoken to them myself. I pictured team members receiving feedback for their work. I visualized the direction in which we would go and used that to define the work to which we would say yes or no.

When the scrutinize phase arrived, visualization was paramount. As the coronavirus pandemic hit during March 2020, my team went to work from home and many of our clients had to close their premises, I visualized how we might get through the turbulence and come out stronger. I pictured myself, in March 2021, telling a friend that the last year had been our best to date. While my inbox and newsfeeds were filling with worried messages, I spoke this pretend conversation out loud. 'After a scary start, everything worked out. We made a plan; we worked together. We pivoted like crazy and didn't just survive – we thrived.'

As I spoke these words, I knew for sure they would come true. Not only did visualization get us through 2020, but it also meant I could show up as an unfazed leader. I could provide the certainty that my team weren't seeing in the media, and it all came true.

Visualization was also my ally during the sale. Once we had commissioned the broker to begin, I wrote a cheque to myself for the sale price I had in mind. In my journal, I mapped out every stage I would encounter during the next six months. I visualized the most relaxed, confident version of me meeting potential buyers and getting on well with them. I imagined the heads of terms arriving, reading it, and confidently nodding, knowing this was the way forward. I pictured sailing through due diligence, enjoying the process and telling my friends. In the end, our sale price was exactly the amount I had written down, and due diligence was a breeze. Not only that, we completed in March 2021 after our best year to date.

Visualization can be a powerful tool. Visualizing the future you want to make happen means that when it happens, it's not a surprise. You've seen it before. It feels familiar and it feels right, and you know exactly what you need to do.

Which deals can you visualize happening? Which contacts can you see coming into your life? Which milestones can you imagine hitting in a big way?

Being exceptional

I deleted her email.

Luckily, she followed up. In October 2016 Yagmur Masmas joined my agency as an intern. Yagmur was a 21-year-old entrepreneur from the Netherlands. She had won a place on an Erasmus-funded exchange programme that placed Dutch entrepreneurs with host businesses in the UK. She had researched carefully and decided she wanted to join my company for six months, hence the email containing this request.

Although work experience is undoubtedly a valuable exercise for graduates, I have found that for employers, it creates a lot of work. Most often, an intern creates more work than they accomplish. They arrive expecting a teacher and a mark scheme and need to be taught from scratch, which is tough for a busy team to accommodate. Over time my agency developed a process for looking after and upskilling work experience students, to mutual benefit, but the learning curve was steep.

Yagmur started as expected. She was quiet and polite; she listened carefully. She made notes in her notebook and got on with her work. While she was typing away with her head down, not disturbing anyone, we almost forgot she was there.

At the end of Yagmur's first week, she and I held a review meeting, with the purpose of seeing how her first week had gone and planning the rest of her time with us. I turned up expecting it to go like many others before, with me asking questions about the week, what she enjoyed and didn't enjoy, what she wanted to explore further, and hearing vague responses in return.

This wasn't what Yagmur had in mind for the meeting.

As soon as I sat down, she handed me a piece of paper with the five-point agenda she wanted to cover, before informing me there would be time for my questions in the allotted FAQ section. She opened the meeting expressing her thanks to me and the team for hosting her and told me she had learned a lot already and was looking forward to the rest of her time with the agency.

Then she moved swiftly through her agenda. Yagmur explained that, having completed all of her tasks beyond the standard expected of her, she had written a list of observations about the office layout and the software programs we used, with some recommendations for my consideration. She had researched 30 of our clients and devised some new ideas for social media campaigns, and she had organized one-to-ones with each account manager over the next two weeks in order that she understand their roles and share her ideas. Her plans over the next six months were laid out on another sheet of paper, and she asked me to review them at my convenience.

'Now it's time for your questions, if you have any,' she concluded. I blinked at her, starstruck.

I had underestimated Yagmur, as had my team. My expectations had been low, and the contrast was blinding. It wasn't just the surprise assertiveness and the handling of the meeting like a seasoned professional; it was the willingness to go above the basics without asking permission and the audacity to barrel forward with what she thought would be useful to us.

In observing, thinking and making efforts to be as helpful as possible, Yagmur had stood out. In not missing anything and thinking a few steps ahead, she had proven herself to be exceptional. Being underestimated hadn't bothered her; it only served to make her even more memorable.

For an entrepreneur, the thread running through each phase – execute, systemize, scrutinize, exit – is being exceptional. Being exceptional buys you autonomy and helps you overcome any 'isms'. What I mean by 'isms' is sexism, ageism, racism and the others. Any prejudice that someone may hold about you can be stopped in its tracks by being exceptional.

When I started my agency, I was fresh out of university and I looked younger than I was. I had no experience in social media apart from having a Facebook account with my university pictures on it. A little girl. I'm sure I was underestimated thousands of times. But I was okay with that. As Yagmur knew, being underestimated gives you the unique opportunity to surprise.

At the core of being exceptional is knowing where to blend in and where to stand out. There's a place for obedience because it buys you autonomy, and you can use your autonomy to do your best work. While there are mavericks and disrupters who are so off the chain and untamed that it's impressive in itself, often their behaviour is so far away from familiar it becomes an unknown and brings scepticism.

Blending in, or being obedient, means doing the basics right. Hitting the standards for what's expected. Turning up on time to meet your clients. Matching their dress code. Shaking hands, looking people in the eye, and remembering their names and interests. Proofreading your emails and being pleased to take clients' calls. These are the basics that check the boxes in someone's mind, provide the familiarity they expect, and meet the standard required for their trust.

Blending in and being obedient win you a reputation for being dependable and steadfast. A solid bet, like the IBM computer or the Harvard grad. But sticking to the path of blending in as an entrepreneur will result in a stagnant journey. Every great entrepreneur has something else about them. They are remarkable. They are exceptional. They stand out.

The premise holds true for employment. The best team members have the most leverage because they have done the fitting in required to build on. Minimum viable normality. Learn the ropes before you change them. Understand the process before you challenge it. Listen to the concerns before bringing your solutions. Approach each encounter with a beginner's mind and be open to learning. It might take a few weeks, it might take a year, but it's an essential stage not to skip. Without the groundwork, potentially brilliant ideas won't be listened to, and you'll be dismissed for not having done the basics or being unrealistic, of bulldozing in without a thorough understanding. Part of playing this game is well-placed obedience, because many people value it.

Once you're owning the basics, build on your foundation as soon as you can, and in many different ways. Look at the options for standing out. You could have the most ideas (which leads to having the best ideas), or you could outproduce everyone else. You could develop an outstanding online presence, blog every day, or start and complete new projects uninitiated. You could understand the clients on a new level, give more than expected, and think of everything.

In the first few years of running my business I often heard about the man with the bow tie. He was an insurance broker. He looked at the other insurance brokers and decided to give himself a memorable gimmick. It worked. The bow tie became his thing, and it was how he was introduced and remembered. He made sure his website ranked for insurance broker bow tie, and the leads came in. The gimmick in itself wouldn't have been enough, but it was backed up by a great service and happy clients, so the message spread.

In college trials the gimmick might be the rugby player with the scrum cap or the orange boots, making selection easy for coaches trying to differentiate players. It's the presenter with a talent for thinking on her feet, or the person doing something a little bit different that sparks the imagination of whoever they tell.

You are remarkable because of what makes you stand out, not blend in. Your strengths lie in your quirks, the unique qualities that only you hold. You might not realize that because the education system, media and herd mentality try to make us uniform.

Your strength is the one-of-a-kind way you write, speak or present. The eye you have for style or detail or bullshit. How calm you stay when others panic. How happy you are during doom and gloom. The way you can make someone feel special when they thought no one noticed, or heard when they felt ignored. No one can compete with you on being you.

Move towards what makes you different. Love it. Embrace it. Be proud of who you are without covering it up or toning it down. Know for sure you're bringing something new, but much needed, to the world.

Stand out by what you say, what you do, the work you put out there, the network you hold, your brand and marketing. Stand out because of your disposition, your ideas, your humility or your quick wit. Stand out because of what people say about you when you're not in the room. Become known for being exceptional.

Only you can decide how you build on being obedient and trusted to become exceptional. There are many options. Find one.

Sliding scales

Entrepreneurs are often thought of as all-or-nothing type people. I know a few who fit that bill. They are either insanely brash or consistently meek. They appear in your inbox multiple times in one week, and then there's nothing for months. They go hard or go home, doing nothing by halves.

Rather than think in terms of extremes, it's useful to think in terms of sliding scales. Here's where entrepreneurs seeking to make a bigger mark in a shorter space of time, akin to a Ten Year Career, can find balance and secure the best of both worlds.

Combining sliding scales with intention means you spend your time deliberately. Your day will feel less like a pendulum, relentlessly swinging between opposites. You'll find a sustainable cadence that fits you perfectly.

One scale runs from manager to maker, where you spend your time managing people (at one end), doing creative work (at the other) or a combination. Combinations can be tricky because they involve strict use of time and boundaries to separate the two. I used to spend my mornings in maker mode and my afternoons in manager mode, which is fine until someone needs you at 9 am. Because my team knew about the scale, and how I used it, they knew my mornings were spent writing and otherwise being unavailable. This set expectations and avoided confusion. It created clarity for them.

Another scale is producer to consumer. The best producers do a little consuming to gather inspiration and establish their tastes, but too much consuming (often under the guise of research) can lead to paralysis by analysis.

Sometimes you will work to a formulaic agenda, and sometimes you'll be happy to follow. Sometimes you'll do what you love; sometimes you'll choose to love what you do. In managing people there's a scale from micromanagement to neglect. Different people require different levels of the scale, a flexible approach.

Because everything you do is on a scale, setting up for success means testing the edges before deciding what is the right balance for you. Rather than registering a trademark, buying a domain name, and sharing your plans for a big change, you might first journal about it and see what comes up. You might test its validity with a few people before sending a mass mailer. In how you spend your time, you might experiment with when you exercise and build up gradually, rather than committing to a fixed regime from day one.

All or nothing might feel right, but acknowledgement of a scale brings intention and choice. You can opt to sit at different parts of a scale depending on which phase of your business you're in.

In my email is a folder named 'Yes but not yet'. It's where I store the opportunities or invitations that don't fit my plans at the time. Where I decide that for the next three months I'll say yes to working on a new book and no to podcasts and speaking gigs. Any podcast or speaking gig invitation receives a polite 'yes, but not yet' response, and I say I'll get back in touch when I am booking podcasts and speaking gigs. If there are opportunities with fixed dates that I will miss by saying no, I'm okay with that. When the time is right, I email them all back, open my calendar and spend a month doing interviews. Non-stop podcasting or no podcasting at all.

I operated at the extreme for a month, and a month only, before deciding what I wanted to do about podcast interviews going forward. It was an enjoyable and useful experiment that I plan to repeat. If I said yes to every podcast interview that arrived and worked solely at the whim of requests in my inbox, I would find myself flitting about. The existence of a scale brings structure and provides a framework within whose parameters I can intentionally choose my way of working.

Unless you question, you agree mindlessly. Unless you define your standards, you accept anything. Unless you know what you want, you follow any path. Unless you can say no, your time will be taken from you. Unless you have boundaries, you are walked all over. Unless you know what you are here to give, you won't get.

Mapping what you do onto scales, defining the extremes, then deciding where you will sit brings purpose and intention to every part of your work. It means you run your business, rather than it running you.

What type of person can do this well? Someone who knows who they are.

Who are you?

Tim came to do work experience as an intern at my agency in the year before it was acquired. Tim showed every promise of being great. He had good ideas and he spoke coherently about them. But Tim let himself down in small ways. He went AWOL when he'd committed to showing up. He turned up late to team meetings and needed to be filled in on the conversation. He would ask for feedback and then not implement it. He rarely produced work without being chased. He was all ears in briefing meetings, only for the flames to die out quickly.

Tim missed the point of the exercise and ended up punching keys on a keyboard until the clock hit five. What started as an opportunity for Tim to establish himself and his network led to no one noticing he was gone. Brand Tim, not great. But Tim had chosen to ask us for work experience. He'd chosen to put himself forward. It was for his benefit; no one forced him to be there.

Tim might say that agency life wasn't for him, but it would be an excuse. Exceptional people bring their best self to every situation, even if they believe it's beneath them. They represent their brand. They aren't too cool to have a go. They give the respect a situation warrants. They don't waste their time or the time of others.

Who are you?

In a professional sense you are a brand. The strength of your brand is the difference between 'She would be great, I'll give her a call' and 'Nah, she's not quite right'. Your brand precedes you. If you're at the helm of a business, you are on show and your brand is your responsibility because only you will give it the seriousness it warrants.

Your people form part of your brand because they represent you. Same with your website. Your social media pages. What you wear and what you say and how you say it all form part of your brand. Others like to feel as if they know you and what you would do in specific situations. It's how they predict what you'll do next or how you might help them.

There are authors who put out title after title and they all become bestsellers. The strength of their brand and the quality of their work have earned the future sales of each new title. They don't have to earn someone's attention again, at least not to the same extent. The power of your brand compounds over time. If someone has always been pleased with your work, you'll be offered the next gig with no pitch. If someone knows you won't let them down, you have their trust going forward.

Movie directors establish their brands in the style of the films they make. Quentin Tarantino has signature moves he uses in each film, and fans delight in spotting them. All my favourite movies happen to have the same director, Christopher Nolan. His use of time travel, disjointed events and concealment of key information until exactly the right moment is something I enjoy in a film. Now I'm first in line to see anything new he creates.

How do you serve and who does it matter to? Who are you and what's your signature style? How do you want to be known? How do you want to be remembered? The answers make up brand you.

The grandma test

How you do anything is how you do everything.

Anonymous

Grandmas are reasonable people and they always see the best in others; mine did. She would listen before asking questions or offering any advice, but she always knew what to do. My grandma became a guardian angel figure in my mind, even before she passed away. I try to channel her kindness into everything I do. Before a conversation I wasn't looking forward to, or when deciding what to do, I'd check if my plan passed the grandma test: could I tell grandma the truth, or would I hide details?

Actor Matthew McConaughey's analogy for the grandma test is crumbs. Crumbs take many forms. They are those people you annoyed that you bump into a few years later. The affair you're having that means you have to hide your phone and be aware of who might be around. The fib you told about what you did at the weekend that now you have to remember. McConaughey doesn't like leaving crumbs.

What reminds you to always do the right thing? The grandma test? Crumbs? Thinking, 'Would I want my kids to do this?' or thinking of yourself as a character in the movie of your life? Everything is a test. How you make choices under pressure or in the midst of a crisis will be what defines you. I often ask myself, 'Will this matter in five years?' Chances are the issue will be long gone but how you dealt with it will remain.

If everything is a test, make your personal policy for how you operate. At my agency we used to imagine there was a client in the room at all times. It was a constant reminder to focus on solutions and avoid pointless grumbles. It required awareness at first, and then it became second nature.

A solid operating framework and a clear sense of right and wrong aren't there so you can judge others. They're not there to moralize your relationships or govern anyone else's behaviour. As author and publisher Louise Hay writes, 'It is arrogant to set standards for others. We can only set standards for ourselves.' You set these standards to guide your way. The goal is to be the example, not to preach it.

Everything is a test. At any given moment you can decide whether you pass it and what passing it even means. You decide whether to be humble or proud, choose kindness or malice, be firm or gentle. You decide whether to say something or keep quiet. You decide whether to call someone out or let it slide. What does the best version of you do? The one you want to become? Act like that person.

Starve the rumour mill

In the early days of networking, I realized that people talk. People really talk. Apart from my close friends or advisors, I came to assume that telling one person would mean telling everyone. I learned to only share things I would be happy with anyone knowing.

There's an episode of *Sabrina the Teenage Witch* I watched with my sister as a kid. In the episode Sabrina has a magic machine: a rumour mill. She can write down a rumour and feed it in, and soon the information becomes something everyone knows. She submits silly rumours and is horrified to find out how fast they spread around school and how mean it is. The episode ends with her only sharing kind rumours about others.

You can decide what will feed the rumour mill and which flames you fan. Louise Hay writes, 'If I hear bad news, I keep it to myself. If I hear good news, I tell everyone.' Are you going to be the spreader of joy or the spreader of gossip and fear? The one who radiates positivity or the one who shares the misfortunes of others? It's a test.

Job versus business

Entrepreneurship is living a few years like most people won't so you can live the rest of your life like most people can't.

Anonymous

My friend Richard commutes for 90 minutes on a packed train to work at a desk in a city centre coworking space. He says he can't exercise because work is too busy. He takes a salary and three holidays every year. He chats with his team over coffee and tries to stay focused on the work he needs to do. He watches until the clock hits five and then he's back on the train home. He hides his laptop away at weekends and doesn't open his emails until Monday morning.

That life sounds common until I tell you that Richard owns the business. If Richard thought about his life and designed it from scratch, would it look like this? Absolutely not. He's been influenced by whatever is normal. He's doing what he sees others do. He's forgetting that he has choices, and he's settled into a pattern. There's no need. Richard has created himself a job with the most demanding boss ever, from whom he can never escape.

You can create a business or you can create yourself a job. To create a business, you have to eliminate the job vocabulary. Thinking of what you do as a job keeps you playing small. Separate from the idea of time in exchange for money and release the notion of a day's work for a day's pay. Being constrained by the normal definitions of work will not work for achieving the Ten Year Career.

You are not here to create yourself a job, and you are not here to sell your time for money. You are not paid a salary, because the amount you can earn is not limited or fixed. You don't book holiday time because you come and go as you please. You are not subject to any of the ways of thinking that a job forces you to use. A Monday morning doesn't have to be any different from a Saturday morning. You can be in the swimming pool at 11 am on a weekday or you can be at your laptop at 8 pm on a Friday night. Arbitrary associations do not serve a Ten Year Career; they serve a career conveyor belt.

Setting boundaries and routines is vital, but you are not going to get what you want following a cookie-cutter pattern of what society thinks a 'job' should look like and the hours you should work. If you want what no one else has, do what no one else does. Thinking of your work as a job is the opposite of autonomy and mastery and it's the opposite of fulfilling your potential. We're not here to create you a job.

Progressing through stages

At the start of 2015 I took a piece of paper and wrote down every single process that happened within my agency. Everything. The lead-generation process, the sales process, the client services process, the invoicing clients and paying suppliers processes. I wrote everything that happened each month in column A. In column B I wrote the name of the person who currently looked after the process. They were all me with a few exceptions. I stared at those two columns of processes that had become my reality and saw the opportunity.

Once I realized I was frazzled, I started to make big changes. I had created myself a job with long hours and many dependencies. I wasn't playing to my strengths because I was fitting too much into my calendar. It was time to create a business.

The theory of comparative advantage, first outlined by David Ricardo in the eighteenth century, helps a country decide which exports to focus on producing. He said that a country stands to gain the most by focusing on the industry where it has the most substantial comparative advantage. For example, even though England and Portugal were both capable of making cloth and wine, England was able to produce better cloth for a lower cost and Portugal the same with wine. Under Ricardo's theory, England should stop producing wine and Portugal should stop producing cloth. Instead, they should trade, bringing benefits to each country. I faced a similar situation in my company. What should I stop doing, and what should I do more of?

The list of tasks marked things that I was doing and had become good at. In economics terms, my task now was to work out which I was comparatively the best at. I needed to find other people who could be comparatively good at that which I no longer wanted to do or knew I shouldn't be doing.

At the top of column C I wrote the heading 'By whom?' and at the top of column D I wrote 'By when?'. A plan was forming. I went through every process and wrote someone else's name in column C. Either someone in my team who I knew would enjoy and be good at the process, or the name of a role that didn't exist, that I would create.

For some of the processes I wrote 'Stop doing'. They were processes that didn't make sense for me or another team member to do. I hadn't realized that, so far, I had been doing them without questioning.

I gave myself a deadline in the fourth column, then closed my eyes, and pictured a world where everything laid out was expertly taken care of by someone else. It felt glorious.

I decided that in the short term I wanted to look after sales, alongside a new sales team member. I wanted to hire great people, and I wanted to make big plans for the agency's future. That was it. In the long term I wanted to have the sales process looked after by someone else, too.

I wanted to focus on midsized clients. They had enough of a budget that we could deliver the service that would make a difference. We knew what size businesses they tended to be, and we knew how to work well with them. Our customer archetype became clear, which gave the sales process more focus because we knew how to prioritize.

I wanted to hire an amazing social media trainer to take over the delivery of sessions. I wanted to empower and upskill my account managers to look after their clients solo.

Where to go seemed so straightforward when I laid it all out; now it was a case of doing it. The middle was messy. I was hiring while spending more time with my team while project work came in and I did all the delivery. My phone still rang all the time. At night I wrote up every process into manuals, which my team helped with. Before long the company had documented ways of doing every process to our standards; high quality and consistent. That meant I could hire, train and hand over.

Staying small means never doing the hard parts of change. Micromanaging means intervening when it gets messy. For me, the only way to reach the glorious part of change was training and trusting. Training and trusting. Over and over again. The right people in the right roles. The right training. Giving the benefit of the doubt. Ensuring they could hit the standards and deliver our processes without being afraid to improve them, then letting them have the autonomy they needed to make their mark.

I knew which new clients we should focus on and I knew what I should focus on. I knew where our standards had to be. The change was a huge challenge, but that year everything stepped up. It started with a simple spreadsheet with four columns. I hadn't skipped any stages; I wasn't trying to delegate anything I didn't know how to do and couldn't teach. The execution part was complete. I had moved from stage one of building a business to the systemize stage; this simple document marked the strategy that would take the company forward.

Determine the playing field. Define your brand. Become crystal clear on your mission and know what you will do to get there. Know who you are and know who you are serving. Develop acute awareness of how your time is being spent and redirect your energy according to what you know is or isn't working. Visit each stage in turn and become hyper-aware of when it's best to execute or refine your strategy. Set up for success in a way that fills you with excitement and gets you raring to go.

Key takeaways

- Recognize where you are in the four main phases of the Ten Year Career: execute, systemize, scrutinize, exit.
- Just be exceptional.
- Become aware of the scales you operate along, and act with intention about where you sit.
- Be mindful and protective of your personal brand.
- Act as if someone is watching your every move.
- Don't simply create a job for yourself. Instead, create a life you love to live.

Serious about your success

Head over to the free *Ten Year Career* companion course for short videos and bonus downloads to apply this chapter's concepts and frameworks to your life and business.
Find it at jodiecook.com/TYC

6

Everything Is Sales

• • •

My friend Will Grant worked as a consultant with software developers who saw sales as a separate department. This frustrated him, so he wrote the following manifesto:

> The most important word in the sentence 'I'm starting a tech business' is business. Stuff that doesn't initially appear to be about sales has a tendency to become about sales.
>
> - Convincing talented people to join you is sales.
> - Securing a business bank account is sales.
> - Getting third-party providers to give you services at a decent rate is sales.
> - Getting press and PR coverage is sales.
> - Convincing your team of your vision is sales.
> - Getting users to use your product is sales.
> - Getting customers to pay for your product is sales.
> - Securing investment from angel investors or VC funds is sales.
>
> If you're great at tech, but not so great at sales – you need to work with someone who is.

While Will's manifesto is about tech businesses, his words apply to any business. Every encounter with anyone is sales. Instead of thinking of 'sales' as scary, think of it as freeing. It's an excuse to be your best self in every scenario. It's less about never letting your guard down and more about being proud of what's under the mask.

Some entrepreneurs love selling, often because they're good at it. They like the chase; they like clinching the deal. However, for many business owners, selling is a necessary evil. It's something they do reluctantly because they fear rejection or they don't want to be pushy. It doesn't have to be that way. Selling is just as much about being a trustworthy, authentic business owner who delivers results as it is about taking learn-to-sell courses and having a slick telephone manner.

Sales matter because, without any customers, you don't have a business. You know this. While there are some examples of acquisitions made of companies with zero revenue, in most cases your investors want a return, your team wants paying and you do, too. Sales solve many problems because when sales are flowing, you can figure everything else out, knowing that what you're putting out there is already resonating and adding value to your audience.

Becoming a person or company that people want to buy from doesn't happen by accident.

In this chapter we up your sales game. I'll explain why consistency is key, why naivety isn't always bad, and why knowing what you want involves rabbits and elephants. We cover strategies for making effortless sales, including solving other people's problems, playing the giving game, and following up to make those sales that will revolutionize your business and supercharge your Ten Year Career.

Naivety

There is a time and a place for naivety. It tends to be talked about as a negative concept used to belittle, but naivety can be one of your biggest strengths.

At Greenfield Print and Promotion, my job was to answer the phone, take orders, find the right supplier for the customer and manage the personalization of the product before it shipped to the customer. When the phone didn't ring, I made calls using any database I could find: previous customers, previous enquiries or online directories.

At the time I didn't realize cold calling was something that many salespeople don't like to do. It was part of my job, so I did it. Many people I called weren't interested, but some would answer my questions, and some turned into quotes and then customers. I quite liked making connections with strangers and turning an initial disturbance into a welcome call.

One day, my boss Simon burst into the office. 'Jodie! Our projections are way out,' he exclaimed. 'You had me thinking we were on for a record year!'

I didn't know what Simon was talking about. I had been diligently following the sales process. A feature of our customer relationship management software, Promoserve, allowed me to assign a percentage chance of each customer placing an order, so I did this after every call or email. Some of the conversations I had were great. I got them excited about their branded mugs, and they were eagerly awaiting the quote in their inbox. They were 100 per cent going to order. Some had to check with someone else or had to think about it, but they still sounded keen. I marked these as 80 or 90 per cent because they might not get approval or they might say no, but I still thought we were in with a good chance.

If someone didn't answer the phone or respond to my emails, I marked them as 60 or 70 per cent because they were probably just busy. If someone told me that they weren't going to proceed, I marked them as 20 or 30 per cent because they might not be happy with their current supplier or they might want something from us in the future. No one was marked zero per cent.

Simon explained that my percentages were all wrong, and he needed to teach me how to use the feature.

The percentages I put into the system threw the forecasts out because I thought every quote had a dramatically higher chance of converting than Simon believed it did. Simon wanted me to reduce the percentages to the company standards.

Even as Simon explained his rationale, I was confused. I thought if someone was calling for a print and promotion quote, they would go ahead with the purchase. I didn't understand why someone would be calling without the intention to buy. Who would do that?

According to Promoserve, this naivety meant I followed people up almost five times as much as the other salespeople. Whenever I logged on to Promoserve I saw rows of potential orders, and I couldn't wait to speak to them. I was way more friendly. Far more helpful. I treated everyone like a valued customer because that's what I believed they were about to become.

In fact, time showed that my results were closer to my optimistic predictions than Simon's seasoned scepticism. So, while I had been naive, my 'naive' actions led to my sales outperforming the norm by a multiple of eight. Remember the questioning mindset? This is another expression of it – why should I, or you, buy into the limitations other people believe?

Even the most seasoned or sceptical seller would benefit from some naivety and blind optimism. The person who believes their sale will happen and the person who believes it won't are both right.

Naivety means not knowing most quotes are duff and following them up anyway. Naivety means not knowing sales are usually down in January and making your calls regardless. Naivety means not knowing that every other agency bills at the end of the month and billing your clients up front. Naivety means being oblivious to industry standards.

Naivety assumes a blank canvas, a clean slate. It means making the best assessment of the present situation and deciding what to do based on that. What worked once might not work again. What didn't work once might work given different circumstances. It's nearly always better to try.

Naivety is not knowing the way it's always been done and doing it the best way instead.

Determining what you want

Independent financial advisors (IFAs) invest in stocks and shares on behalf of their clients, charge fees on winnings (and transactions), and take their clients to play golf. Vanguard, on the other hand, is an online trading platform that lets individuals invest without a traditional broker. Vanguard sells stocks, shares and index funds but won't schmooze you over dinner. It charges far lower fees because it has invested in technology and can serve many people at scale.

You can sell your house using an estate agent. You instruct them, and they visit to take pictures for their website and shop window. They take people round when you're not there, and they negotiate on your behalf. They take sizeable commissions for doing so. UK online estate agent Purplebricks lets you take pictures of your property, list it on their system with all the details, and then show selected buyers around yourself. The buyers bid online, and you choose which offer you accept. The fees are smaller because you do the work.

Part of knowing what you deliver and the difference it makes for others is deciding who it's for. Your product or service can leave someone underwhelmed or delighted, depending on how well matched they are. If anyone can become your client, anyone will become your client. This might mean you attract clients who aren't your ideal customer, requiring you to adapt your offering or provide a suboptimal service. If you've ever regretted taking on a client, it's likely they weren't the kind you were meant to serve. Maybe you underdelivered in a sector you were unfamiliar with. Maybe your expectations were totally misaligned with your client's. Maybe there was a cultural or values mismatch between your teams.

Those ill-fitting clients take the place of your dream clients, and they invite their friends, and soon your business is associated with a non-ideal client base. If you're intentional, however, you can choose which clients you work with. Who do you want to serve and who are you best placed to serve? What game do you want to play and with whom?

There are three types of clients: rabbits, deer and elephants. The simplistic hunting analogy says that rabbits are everywhere. They are easy to catch, there isn't much meat on them, but when you catch a few and look after them, your rabbit clients introduce their rabbit friends, and your collection of rabbits will multiply.

Deer are in the middle. They take one person to catch, but they can feed a family for a week or so. You have to keep an eye out to spot them, but once you know how, you can catch plenty of deer.

Elephants are at the other end of the spectrum. They are harder to catch, and it might take more than one person to capture one. They can sustain a family for years once caught. Having only one elephant, however, means if someone steals your elephant or it runs away, you'll need to catch another one.

Your strategy could involve capturing rabbits, deer and elephants simultaneously, but that comes with drawbacks. They need different equipment. A rabbit trap won't catch an elephant. A team trained in spotting and finding deer is wasted on rabbits. Plus, once you've captured all three, they need different treatment. They require different handling. Elephants don't like being treated like rabbits. They don't like being squeezed into small places and they will kick up a fuss and make a lot of noise if not given the right attention.

Going after rabbits might work for you. It involves being good at capturing rabbits in such a way that they multiply. In a business sense, this means an app or platform that can serve many people at a time. It's robust processes that stand up to volume. It's ideas that spread, or small yet essential purchases that are readily available. Rabbits aren't suited to every business and they might not be right for yours, especially if the frictional or management cost of serving every client is high.

Going after deer can be a solid strategy that requires a strict and precise technique. It involves team-agreed standards of what constitutes a deer. What about zebras and antelopes and alpacas? They're about the same size – do they get in? It requires the right tools to catch and serve. In a business sense, this means laser-sharp focus and a way of operating that suits this type of customer.

Elephant hunting is fruitful once your process is mastered. When you've set up how you'll store the elephant once you have him, you might find that catching elephants becomes your jam. You can do it again and again, and you realize that you can sustain not only yourself and your family but an entire village. The possibilities are endless.

You might look at your own business now and instinctively know which customers it is best placed to serve. That may or may not be who you actually are serving. No matter how far along your journey you are, you can always determine what you want from here onwards. Establishing what you want is far easier once you know who you are, what you stand for and what you're here to give. It might hit you like a lightning bolt in the middle of the night. Yes! This is what I want.

Although my hunting metaphor may be clear cut, real life is not always. Some of the most disruptive businesses are successfully treating rabbits like elephants by providing a first-class service at scale. Or they are seeing with elephants the economies of scale that normally come with rabbits, making complicated transactions simple without compromising quality.

Businesses that struggle to find their client fit may have mismatched tools for different types of client, or they don't home in on a particular type. Businesses that do well work out exactly how to catch rabbits, deer or elephants in consistent ways. They define their clients and serve their needs in a way that works at scale, no matter the type of customer.

Knowing and serving your perfect client may unlock harmony and growth like you've never experienced.

Meeting people

In the early days of running an agency, I attended a weekly networking event. Fifty members met to update each other on their businesses and who they wanted to be introduced to.

Each Thursday's event had a section in which each member had one minute to take the mic and address the room. Some of the members used the time to plug their special offers and drum up orders there and then. They saw the other members as their potential customers and tried to get them on board. Others saw it differently.

Those 50 people were each going about their week meeting new people. If each member met three new people each week, that meant 150 new people in my extended network, every single week.

I saw those 50 people as my business friends and my extended sales team, and treated the information I included in my one-minute slot accordingly. My method at this event, or any event for that matter, is not to sell to the room, it's to sell through the room. To be so remarkable during my 60-second slot that the other members remembered me all week. To entertain, to surprise, to make them laugh. To bring my best self to each meeting and become known for my integrity and credibility.

Tracing back my agency's next 20 clients to the source, I found that over half of them had arrived as a result of those 50 people in my Thursday-morning networking group. Some were direct referrals, and some were connections of someone I had met through the group. Selling through the room, not to the room, was a long-term strategy that worked.

Seeing the members as potential customers was a short-sighted approach that frustrated those who attempted it. Fifty people all buying from each other wouldn't make business sense; it would create a bubble. Plus, selling to your friends is cringeworthy and means they start to avoid you. If they want to buy, let them, but treat with caution.

The growth of your business is proportionate to the number of people who feel they know, like and trust you. The more people who know you, the more people whose minds you are in, the more you can spread your message and the more you can give. Every single person you meet is a chance to make an impression. Every person you meet can be someone you keep in touch with for ever. Most initial referrals for a company's first few sales come from personal connections. Friends of friends. The more people who know, like and trust you, the more people are acting as your sales team when you don't even know it.

Solving someone's problems

Before my first networking event, my summer job boss Simon taught me his method. He said I should arrive early and obtain the attendee list beforehand. This meant I could find my ideal customers and hunt them down (to continue with the analogy). He recommended that I say hi to them first, because not everyone has the confidence to do that. With everyone I spoke to I was to have one goal: find their problem and solve it.

He had been doing this for years and built a successful business. Everyone seemed to know him wherever we went. He had solved so many problems for so many people that they told each other about him, and his efforts multiplied. I listened.

To find and solve someone's problem, Simon talked to them until he discovered something they needed, wanted or were struggling with. Perhaps their partner's birthday was coming up and they wanted a unique gift. Perhaps they were looking for a loo roll supplier. Whatever it was, that was the chance Simon took. He heard their problem and told them that he had a great recommendation. He promised to email it over and asked them for a business card. At the time, most people carried business cards. He took a pen, wrote his follow-up task on the back, and he stored them in the same pocket until he got back home. If they didn't have a business card, he wrote their name, email address and the promise he had made in his notebook.

When Simon returned from the networking event, he worked through the cards. He emailed each person to say how great it was to meet them. He sent the contact details of the person he had promised to introduce or the link he had promised to send. They always responded, and he was forever known as the person who had helped.

His method led to having coffee with new people and them asking if he sold a specific branded product, to which the answer was always yes. He didn't hassle people and he didn't use their data to send promotional mailouts; he just used the method as a way of meeting people and helping them, which he knew would come back around.

Simon knew this was an exercise worth his time. He learned that giving without expectation led to getting.

The giving game

Thousands of candles can be lit from a single candle, and the life of the candle will not be shortened.

Siddhartha Gautama, The Buddha

Nothing was too much trouble for Mark.

I was three years into running my agency and Mark was my mentor. He had built and sold a chain of well-known accessory stores. He always had someone he could call upon for a favour. Whatever he wanted, he could ring someone and they would sort it out for him. At first, I didn't understand how.

Mark spent his career treating people well. He brought out the best in his team members and looked after them. He made introductions and put in good words. He asked great questions and gave stellar guidance. Mark's door was always open, and he always knew someone who could help. It felt as though he was always on your team, cheering you on. Mark had built up a giant favour bank, where he could ask anyone he knew for an introduction or a hand with something and it would always be a yes. They felt like they owed him something, but he didn't see it that way.

His giving nature rubbed off on me, and I started to do the same. Every time someone introduced a friend and they turned into a client, we sent cupcakes to say thanks. I gave out my books and I made introductions. I passed along information that I thought others might find useful. My agency ran 'second opinion' email newsletters in which we offered anyone in our network a free second opinion on a social media campaign or profile. We made a calendar of 'international awareness days' that our audience loved.

I soon found that the more I gave, the more I received. The more I gave favours, kindness, thank-you gifts and help to those around me, the more reciprocations happened. And regularly, too. Invitations would turn up in the mail and my inbox from people who said they were repaying favours. Thanks for that book you gave me, I loved it. Thanks for listening that time, I needed it. Thanks for mentioning my work in your article, it made all the difference. People would pop up to share my work on social media or introduce me to someone they knew. Someone nominated me for the Forbes 30 Under 30 list based on a favour I'd given years before, one that I had forgotten.

Business consultants looked at my agency's webinars, extensive blog posts and everything we did to help our network, and said that we gave too much away, but I never believed it. The more we gave, the more we got. Attendees of our webinars would email us afterwards and ask for a quote. They put our names forward in response to requests on LinkedIn; they introduced their friends and sent colleagues along. Giving away our best knowledge and insights led to commissions to implement and advise, again and again. No one else understood because they were so focused on taking.

It felt like I'd tapped into some magical source of miracles, and I truly started to believe I was being guided along this game. Like my mentor Mark, I wasn't giving to receive; it just happened. I don't think it would have had the same effect had I been keeping score.

Giving works on an abundance mindset rather than a scarcity mindset. Giving doesn't take anything away from me. Compliments, gifts, favours, introductions – they multiply rather than subtract. Whatever I gave came back to me in scores, and I trusted the outcome even if I didn't know the method.

There are so many ways of giving, sharing good vibes, and being synonymous with positivity. The simplest way is to say thanks. Rarely does someone progress through life or business without help from others. Go back in your journey and list those key individuals who did you a favour, gave you a leg-up or introduced you to someone when they didn't need to. Once you start writing, you likely won't be able to stop. Start at the top and say thank you to each person. Drop them an email, pick up the phone, write them a card. Show your appreciation and gratitude for how they helped you. Aim to give a warm and fuzzy feeling to every single name. Be the person who actually said thanks.

Think about your suppliers. Who do you work with that you couldn't do without? Who makes your phone ring, keeps your website secure or ensures your operations are running? Make a list of your best suppliers, past or present, and spread good vibes. Leave them a public review, unprompted. Pay their invoices ahead of schedule. Ask if there's anyone you can introduce them to. Find out what they're working on so you can keep your eyes peeled for opportunities. Become the favourite client of your favourite suppliers by taking an interest in how they're doing.

Whoever you are, you have gifts. Something that seems ordinary to you that is ground-breaking to someone else. Perhaps it's the formula you created for measuring specific outcomes, or the strategy to better manage a team, or the tools you use to stay focused. It might be years of tacit knowledge about a certain subject that you can recall from memory but someone else would have to research for hours.

Find out what your gifts are and work out a way of giving them away. Put them into resources, books, downloads and recordings, and help as many people as you can. Sharing does not divide, it multiplies. Become known, liked and trusted by sharing, helping and giving out your gifts.

Giving does not mean you sacrifice anything; thinking in that way is not conducive to success. Being the person who solves a problem, presents an idea or sparks a new way of thinking is powerful and can result – somehow – in you getting back what you gave with ease. Give, give and give some more, and let getting be an afterthought.

With anything we gave, we were curious about where it went. Finding out the impact of your gifts for their recipients is valuable information that you can use to inform what you continue to give. Now, my favourite emails to receive are from those who have implemented something that I wrote, and made a huge, positive change in their lives. Following up, therefore, should come after giving.

Following up

In the 1990s the UK postal service the Royal Mail ran a series of advertisements with the slogan 'I saw this and thought of you'. The adverts showed people spotting obscure items that they knew their friend would love and mailing them one. When the friend appeared on screen, it was obvious how fitting the item was. Following up well means keeping in touch and remembering things about others. It means finding excuses to reach out, looking for 'I saw this and thought of you' opportunities. It means remembering what you talked about and what's important to them. Their partner's name, what they're working on and what they're struggling with.

If you're present online, or if you own a phone, you can add people on LinkedIn, follow them up, email them, follow them on Twitter. You can take every opportunity to keep in touch with someone, but it doesn't happen by accident.

Successfully following up means having a process that you make happen. It means deciding how and when you're going to ask for contact information. Deciding how you're going to reach out. Deciding when it's appropriate. Not being too proud to be first. Doing so successfully online requires being great online. How you come across has to be stronger because you are not physically in front of someone – but mastering putting yourself out there online has infinite possibility. It's the same process but on a different scale. The more you get to know the people you meet, and the audience you have online, the stronger your network.

Some advice I heard about meeting people was to imagine everyone has a sign above their head saying, 'Make me feel special'. Doing so happens when you take a genuine interest in everyone you meet and invest in the relationship over the long term. You don't have to network, but you do need a consistent way of meeting people and keeping in touch. Work out what you can give, and give it.

Many business owners don't think this applies to them. They think they don't need to meet new people. That's nothing but a limiting belief that leads to stagnation and costs growth.

Valuable interactions and transactions with new people you have met and helped might not happen straight away. Creating a process for following up and staying on someone's radar secures future moments where they need the exact product or service that you offer. Meeting people is the easy part; the hard part is sticking in their mind. The magic is in the follow-ups.

Some business owners hold limiting beliefs about following up. They think that following up is beneath them or (mistakenly) think the right buyers won't need following up. Some are scared of hassling prospects. But even the most oversubscribed businesses have systems in place for keeping in touch. There's just no point giving potential clients the silent treatment.

For the success of your giving game and subsequent follow-ups to be backed by evidence, not reduced to anecdotes and vague feelings, incorporate tracking in your business.

Tracking

As part of the sales process at my agency, we tracked the source of our customers. We could always see the data on the sales system. How are people finding us? What is working and what needs more energy? We wrote as much detail as we could about the source, including which event, which ad, or even which search term they used to find our website. While collecting and recording data took extra effort, we saw it as super-valuable information that could be used to inform future activity.

New customers coming from organic Google searches means your website ranks for commercial terms. Customers from social media means your ideas are spreading and your message is reaching the right people. Customers from certain directories or networks might indicate a good fit between your audience and theirs. New clients coming from physical networking and online networking means your efforts in that area are bearing fruit. New customers coming from paid advertising means your ads are resonating with an audience and compelling them to act.

New customers coming from existing clients means your product or service is suiting them well. If your clients aren't referring their friends, there's likely a problem with your service or product, not your sales team. You may have a churn rate eating into all the new business you win.

The percentage of new customers arriving from client referrals should grow steadily as your client base grows. Without your marketing efforts leading to customers referring more customers, you face an expensive way to run a business that likely won't be sustainable in the long term. Relying on marketing is not enough; people must tell their friends or buy from you again, ideally both. Over time this reduces your marketing costs to zero.

Once you have a breakdown of where your clients come from, work out the percentages of each. New business might be 20 per cent client referrals, 30 per cent Google Ads, 10 per cent social media, 20 per cent referrals from your network and 20 per cent organic SEO. Then think about your time and how you spend it to draw trends. Is your biggest source of new customers such a large percentage because you spend energy on it, or is it a large percentage in spite of not spending energy on it?

Wherever you put your energy and attention will grow. It's true for the sources of your customers, and it's especially true for the most important way of getting new customers – being exceptional for your current clients. If you're not sure where to focus, start there.

Humans are consistent

Following up, arriving on time, respecting other people by not cancelling or postponing commitments – it's not a separate department, it's all sales.

Humans are largely consistent; seemingly inconsequential quirks can speak volumes. If someone turned up to an interview late, unprepared and unresearched, you would reasonably assume that they apply the same sloppy nature to their work, and you wouldn't offer them the role.

Sales includes not letting people down or taking liberties. Your clients are interviewing you through the same lens, and everything you do, whether it's emails without typos or remembering their preferences, forms part of their assessment of whether or not to buy from you.

If you become known as someone of integrity, who does what you say you will, the sales will arrive. If you hold yourself to higher standards, your customers will trust you to look after their business, and you will make sales.

Nailing your sales processes might be the difference between a stagnating business and a flourishing one. Forecast your business growth if you had 50 per cent more leads each week. What about if you converted 30 per cent more prospects into paying clients? What if each new client spent an additional 10 per cent with you? These compounding effects make a huge difference over a matter of years.

Next, we'll look at developing a sustainable structure and way of working, so that your success isn't left to chance.

Key takeaways

- Remember that everything is sales.
- Bring a naive questioning mindset to your work.
- Decide: am I chasing rabbits, deer or elephants?
- Meet as many people as you can.
- To open doors, find and solve other people's problems.
- Play the giving game and follow up.
- Pay attention to how people find you.

Sales solves all

Head over to the free *Ten Year Career* companion course for short videos and bonus downloads to apply this chapter's concepts and frameworks to your life and business.

Find it at jodiecook.com/TYC

7

Hope Is Not A Strategy

• • •

Candice looked fantastic and she felt it, too. She returned from summer weighing two-thirds of what she had before. She had a newfound confidence and was always smiling. Her friends, and friends of friends, all asked how she had done it. Was it a juice diet or intermittent fasting? Did she cut out carbs? What was the hack?

Candice knew the crowd that circled round her wanted to know her trick, and she played up to it. She beckoned to gather them in closer and spoke in a hushed voice. 'Well... don't tell anyone my secret... but...' she built up the tension.

'I started exercising and stopped eating so much.'

In most cases, including Candice's, input equals output. Strategy is choosing which inputs are likely to lead to the desired outputs. It's obvious. If you don't prepare lunch, you'll get hungry and overeat later, or buy something quick from the shop. If you don't prepare for the meeting, you risk not being able to answer a question you should know the answer to. If you hire the wrong person because you're in a rush, it creates more work for the rest of the team.

You can't sleepwalk your way to success. It doesn't happen by accident. A strategy of hope is a strategy of failure.

Picture a white line on a chalkboard, representing a career's upward path over time. At a glance it looks like a solid line, but when you zoom in you see that it's made up of thousands of tiny, scattered dots. The dots are the great days, the breakthrough conversations, the moments of excellence. The times when you focused instead of procrastinating or heard a view that caused a change. The dots are the wins, the lessons, the right decisions. They represent consistent and intentional actions. The specks that group together cause progress in the right direction, the result of which is career and life changing.

On its own each dot looks insignificant, but when viewed together the trajectory is clear. The moments make up the days, which make up the weeks and the months and the years. Life lived a moment at a time is a life made much of.

Moving forward with intention is the difference between having a Ten Year Career and having the same year, ten times.

In this chapter we make intentionality your sustainable default because hope is simply not a strategy for the progress you seek. We assess the value of your time, create habits that compound, and visit consistency, ideas and policies. We cover building a solid team and creating robust feedback loops, while making it all look easy.

Time is a finite resource

From the moment you are born your time ticks away until you die. Death is the only certainty, and yet so many of us kill our time. We waste it, we bide it, we do anything other than grab it with both hands and make the absolute most of every second. The number of dots on your chalkboard is finite. In ten years there are 3,652 days – that's 58,432 waking hours.

To stop acting like we're going to live for ever we need to keep time at the forefront of our minds and be aware of its value. Like the tactics for perspective from Chapter 4, find a way of remembering that your time here is finite and watch how little you waste. This attitude is not meant to be morbid or cause worry, it's meant to be freeing. In the end nothing matters, so you might as well do what you can with everything you've got, including the time available.

You could think about 'the dash', and what you want it to represent. The dash is the small line on your gravestone between the year you are born and the year you die. You could wear a death day watch – it looks like a normal watch but it counts down the seconds to your death day. Only problem is, no one knows when that is. Perhaps you set it at the date of your 80th birthday. What makes you think you'll be that lucky?

Derek Sivers thinks of his time as being worth $500 an hour and considers this for every decision. He's not keen on television series and once worked out that the 63 hours of *Game of Thrones* aired so far at that point represented a cost of $31,500 to watch. Not worth it.

Ingvar Kamprad was the founder of IKEA. His method for success was simple: 'Divide your life into ten-minute units and sacrifice as few as possible in meaningless activity.' What constitutes meaningless activity? You get to know that from studying your actions in terms of cause and effect.

During 2014, when I was working on sales for JC Social Media as well as delivering training sessions and managing a growing team, what I was doing didn't make sense. I should have been focusing on systemizing, but I couldn't let go of execution. I was holding the company back. I knew what I could secure during a day of working on sales, but for every day I was booked, I couldn't do that. I was needlessly busy and needed to make a plan, as I described in Chapter 5.

Once you know which of your actions lead to your business growing, you have a good idea of where your time is best spent. Not only that, you will also know the opportunity cost of doing anything else. Decisions around which roles to hire and what to do next start to become crystal clear. What are you doing that someone else, once trained, could do? Keep delegating and automating until you are doing what only you can do.

There is always a way of acquiring more money, finding great people, solving any puzzle you can dream of by asking the right person the right question or googling it. But time can flitter away without you realizing until you look back and see how much of it you wasted. Master your time and you master everything.

Self-awareness is the biggest deterrent to procrastination. My manager Simon wasn't doing the same thing at events month in, month out, because he had fallen into a routine. He was doing it because it worked. He knew it worked because he tracked its success.

Working out how to spend your time is key, because when your time is spent intentionally you don't waste it. You know what you're there to do and you are rarely sidetracked. Work is personal. How you should spend your time comes from self-awareness, not advice. Every entrepreneur has a different definition of hustle, of a lifestyle business, of working too much or being busy. One person's hustle is another's lifestyle business. One person's hard work is another's flow. One person's too busy is another's just right.

Whatever you call it, find out which inputs yield outputs and drop the nice-to-haves. If where you put your energy isn't translating into the needle moving, even by a small amount, reassess how you spend your time.

Protect your time from time thieves just as you would your laptop or jewellery. Don't become your own time thief; cultivate heightened awareness of what you're doing in every stage of your business. Be aware of when your lizard brain, moving you towards gossip, fear and procrastination, is stealing from you.

Being acutely aware of how important time is means practising how to say, 'I'll leave you to it' or 'I'm going to go now', and then doing what you say. Learn how to get to the crux of an issue without spending hours thinking of solutions to the wrong problems.

The opportunity cost of your time is everything else you could be doing while it's spoken for. It's the tipping point I reached in my agency. We were booking training sessions, and I was delivering them. We were signing clients, and I was their main point of contact. We were receiving enquiries, and I was handling them. Some of the enquiries we received were from exciting prospects, as were the introductions and referrals that hit my inbox almost daily. I knew I was too busy to give them the attention they warranted. I knew I had no chance of converting them into clients without getting to know them, understanding their company and needs, and demonstrating that we could deliver. I realized this was where my time would be best spent. This is how I would grow my company.

Ducking out of responsibilities in favour of recruiting and training someone else to do them is a necessary step that allows the Ten Year Career to happen. But many business owners put it off, or don't do it at all. It might be the owner who does too much paperwork, runs their own social media or follows up unprofitable work. It's not always clear cut. Understand what you do that no one else can do and where your time is best spent, and consider opportunity cost when saying yes to any request.

I had to start valuing my time higher, and to bring on other people to help grow the company. I hired a social media trainer to train our clients, both old and new. I reapportioned this time into upskilling my account managers to communicate better with their clients and take over the meetings, phone calls and report making. I automated parts of the prospecting process, added more fields to our website enquiry form to better vet prospects, and started recruiting for a sales support role.

Time is our only finite resource, so we have to find other resources on which to rely. When I switched from working *in* my business to working *on* my business there was no going back. No more undervaluing myself. Are you the bottleneck to your company's growth? Let's get intentional about how you spend your time.

Making excellence a habit

Ben Banks is the founder of SBD Apparel, the initialism standing for squat, bench, deadlift. It's a prominent brand in strength sport. SBD sponsors the World's Strongest Man and makes knee sleeves that strength athletes wear to train and compete. In an interview Banks shared what he was most and least likely to say at work: most likely to say, 'Let's just check'; least likely to say, 'That will do.' Every product that leaves the SBD warehouse is checked for quality multiple times, in a series of tests designed by Banks and his team.

What's the alternative? Shipping shoddy products and hoping that customers don't return them? The SBD focus is on creating quality products fit for training and competing. The tests ensure that happens.

The standards to which you hold yourself will be the standards emulated by your team. They will mirror you. Make the reflection something worth seeing.

When you hold exceptional people to high standards, they will love working to reach them. They will relish feedback and appreciate opportunities to improve. When that feedback is two-way, each holds the other accountable and it's powerful. Hayley, my agency's business development officer, and I had an agreement. If either of us spotted the other had made a typo, we would tell them. On a proposal, in our customer relationship management (CRM) software, in an email. We pointed them out to each other, which forced us to check before hitting send on anything. I'm grateful that Hayley played along with my game, and I know we both benefitted from it.

During powerlifting competitions, lifters take to the platform to perform a lift they have performed thousands of times before. The goal is to execute each lift to the required standards, the same or better than you can in training. Many powerlifters save their personal best attempts for competitions because the crowd support and adrenalin help them perform better.

When competing in any strength sport, every lift counts. Every time someone performs a squat, their brain fires neurons that remember how to do it. What starts as a conscious process becomes unconscious. Whatever is repeated will soon stick and become second nature. Practice makes permanent. If squats carried out in training aren't to the depth required in the rulebook, or bad habits creep in at heavy loads, they will happen on the platform.

When the stakes are high and the refs are watching, it's impossible to override years of training a specific way. Mistakes in training show when performance counts the most. The only option is to pretend you are competing every time you train. Assume that there are no dress rehearsals and that everything is a test. Remember that how you do anything is how you do everything, and act accordingly.

It's far better to make excellence a habit than pray that when the pressure is on excellence will fall into place.

In his book *Atomic Habits*, James Clear takes a comprehensive look at habits. He makes the case for systems versus goals. Systems consisting of actions that happen first consciously, then unconsciously, and finally form habits. We already know that humans have mostly the same thoughts each day, but we do the same things each day, too.

The rules of habits as told by Clear are: (1) make it obvious; (2) make it attractive; (3) make it easy; and (4) make it satisfying. Set up good habits by crafting your day to ensure the habits you want to instil fulfil these four rules. Make it obvious by putting your journal on top of your laptop or laying out your running kit, so it's clear what you need to do. Make it attractive by promising yourself a certain reward on completing a certain number of days of the habit. Make it easy by moving the biscuit tin away from the coffee machine, or not having a biscuit tin altogether. Make it satisfying by creating milestones that you tick when complete, or reflection periods where you look back at the habit and what it led you to achieve.

Without habits, every problem is solved like it's happening for the first time.

Starting good habits is harder than maintaining good habits because starting requires making a plan, executing it and calling on willpower for the first few times. Once the habit is embedded, willpower is surplus to requirements. Marathon runners don't unwittingly drag themselves out of bed for every training run; they simply carry out a habit. Same with writers who publish book after book: the writing practice is a habit. Maintenance mode is the place to be.

Keystone habits are beyond habits. They are the foundation routines and practices by which someone operates. They mark the base level of what you do without any need for willpower or persuasion. The default. Whether positive or negative, each keystone habit has a ripple effect across everything you do.

If every time you see your family you argue, if every piece of work you submit is shoddy, and if your conversations revolve around gossip, these habits will have a negative effect on other areas of your life. Arguments lead to resentment; subpar work leads to lower financial return; gossiping leads to wasting time and becoming a judgemental person. It's easy for bad habits to spiral.

Do not underestimate the power of habits and their compounding benefits. They will forge the culture and identity of your business and how it's perceived by others. Remove chance, remove the need for willpower and make excellence the minimum standard.

If every day you spring up to your alarm, make your bed and say something nice to yourself in the mirror, you've already carried out three keystone habits that have set up your day. Your wake-up routine is likely having positive ripple effects on everything else you do. Nothing happens in a vacuum.

Identify your keystone habits. What are those routines, practices and behaviours that you do (or don't do) without thinking? Maybe you always go to bed at a certain time, or plan your week every Sunday, or journal every evening, or always say no to a second drink. Perhaps you reread every email before sending to check for tone and typos. Write a long list of these habits and then assess what the list says about you. Imagine you were given that list and told it described the behaviour of someone else. What predictions would you make for their future?

Assessing where you are means you can be intentional about which habits should no longer be part of your life and begin new ones that will alter your trajectory. Some people need to hit rock bottom before they make meaningful changes, but that can be avoided with foresight and planning.

In 2020 the world changed. The UK went into lockdown on 23 March and its citizens didn't know how long it would last. Listening to the prime minister addressing the nation, I thought about what my days were going to look like. No working from coffee shops, no travelling to an office, no travelling at all – no weekend trips away or venturing abroad. No seeing friends or family, no going out for dinner. Although gyms had to close, my gym loaned its kit to members in return for them keeping their memberships going, so luckily, I had a barbell and some weights.

With all those aspects of my regular life taken out, I thought about what remained. My apartment, my laptop and Kindle were intact. Groceries were being delivered. Time was on my side. I looked at my calendar in awe of how much blank space remained once I removed all my plans. What would I do with this time? The lockdown wasn't a problem. It was an opportunity.

I knew that how I spent the first week of lockdown would likely be how I spent its duration. I didn't fancy waiting around for it to be over. I didn't fancy slipping into bad habits. Instead, I created a 30-day challenge to try to instil some new, different habits that would make the most of all this time I now had.

On a piece of paper divided into 30 days, I wrote ten things I wanted to do every day, to tick when complete. The list included reading, writing, doing a Daily Calm, taking a walk, and speaking to someone who inspires me. Some of the items I already did, albeit sporadically and when I could fit them in. Now I had no excuses. During the first week I left most until the end of the day and then rushed to complete them before bedtime, but soon I did them earlier and earlier. Soon they became embedded not just as habits but as priorities.

The 30-day habit checklist is now something I do every month. It's progressed from a piece of paper to a spreadsheet, I've got my husband involved, and some of the habits change each month. Some, like going for a daily walk, no longer need to be on there. The practice changed my life within one month, and a year later it's unrecognizable. Writing down daily habits that the best version of me did automatically, and repeating them until willpower wasn't required, was the firepower I needed to get through 2020 and come out stronger.

Lockdown or no lockdown, it starts with a list of what the best version of you does every single day.

I want to have my errors pointed out by people who care. I want to hear critique, take it on board and keep improving in every area of my work. As a business owner it can be difficult to find someone who will call you out, especially if you pay their wages. Empowering your team to do so will flatten the organization and show your commitment to upholding the standards you teach.

Determine where standards should be higher by identifying weaknesses in your business. If I gave your closest competitor £10 million to crush you, what would they do? Whatever they would attack is what to strengthen. Proactivity is always better than reactivity, especially where standards come in.

In order for a customer to build a positive impression of you in their mind, take them through a series of exceptional touchpoints. This might be the way you greet them, the user experience of your website, the proposal design, or the welcome gift they receive. It could be how well you remember what they tell you. In your business what are the touchpoints someone might encounter along their journey to working with you and how can you make each exceptional?

Focus

Imagine you were about to take a walk, and I told you there were lots of wonky paving slabs around. Chances are, on that walk that's what you'd notice. You'd likely spot many and come back to say, 'Yes, you were right, there were loads.' Or how about if I said, 'Today's a great day for a walk. The temperature is perfect and the sky is beautiful'? Your experience would be totally different. Same walk, different focus.

Whatever you focus your attention on expands. Focus on what's broken and that's all you'll see. Focus on what's right and you see more of it. If you focus on growth, you grow. If you focus on family, your family life improves. It's the same for health and fitness and any aspect of work. Focus channels energy in the direction you are looking. So where are you looking?

When welcoming visitors into my agency's offices, we noticed where their focus was. Some would comment on our bright and airy office, then tell us about the big plans they had for their business. Others would tell us how hard it was to find a parking space, then disclose which competitors they were trying to beat.

Close friends of focus are purpose and flow. Enemies of focus are distractions and whatever anyone else is doing. Focus is honed by 30-day challenges but also by deciding what you will not focus on.

Having a Ten Year Career requires opting out of most things to focus on what matters. Cultivating selective ignorance is a skill, as is practising indifference. Opting out takes strength because it requires defying peer pressure, and at school we were trained to fit in. Standing out was not a good thing because it made you different. Opting out requires perspective. If all your mates obsess over football scores, you'll need to zoom out to think about the role you want football to play in your life. Without zooming out or taking a stance, we lose focus because we follow the focus of others.

In year five of my Ten Year Career I began working from a different country for one month in every three. Two months in the UK, one away. Repeat. I minimized my possessions and kept only what was essential to the life I wanted to lead, while away or at home. The television went to charity. I knew it was not part of my best existence and chose to be indifferent to popular television series. Opting out took strength when I found myself in conversations where everyone had watched the same show. But then I got over it. Now, if someone asks me if I've seen something, I say no, we talk about something else, and it's no big deal. Over time they remember, and we use different conversation topics.

Perhaps you are proud to never watch the news, know nothing of the songs in the charts or are unable to name a Kardashian. Maybe you cultivate selective ignorance of other people's bad driving or workplace drama. Or you opt out of judging and forming opinions, and your life is better for it.

Focusing on making good habits and chunking good days together expands. Being proudly indifferent to that which makes no difference is the powerful edge to your strategy of focus.

Consistency

The one thing that great morning routines have in common is that they are consistent. A question I asked on Twitter about morning routines had over a hundred responses from entrepreneurs who couldn't wait to tell me theirs. Some people work first, some exercise, some read a book, some have breakfast with their family. Different contents, but the routine was there. They had assessed their options and decided their plan.

There's a reason why the leaders of impressive companies often have a uniform, the same few outfits they always wear. A uniform removes the need for a decision first thing in the morning. Perhaps they eat the same meal for breakfast and lunch, removing the need to decide. Decision fatigue is real, so they save the energy for those decisions that matter.

The *5 AM Club* introduces the concept of a victory hour, which I love. Your victory hour is the first hour of each day. The concept says that spending this hour well sets up a great day, over which you have control. You control your input and your disposition, and it leads to mastery and ownership and focus with daily consistency. During lockdown I coupled my 30-day challenge with the concept of a victory hour. I completed specific items on my challenge during my first waking hour, and each time I felt like I'd won the day before breakfast.

It's ridiculous and unsustainable to fit in meditation, yoga, a run and focus work within the first hour of every day, but it's not ridiculous or unsustainable to do a few of those things consistently, until they become habits. It's not ridiculous or unsustainable to remove everything else from your victory hour, such as the news, social media, or your phone in general.

Focus and consistency require making decisions. Remember, the word 'decide' etymologically means 'to cut away'. Cut away the non-essential in favour of the essential. Cut away everything you could do in favour of what you will do.

Finding consistency requires being aware of your energy levels throughout the day. Know when you work best, which foods, projects and people give you energy or drain you, and incorporate this into your daily practice and your victory hour.

Cadence

It is obvious that regular training sessions give incomparably greater effects than episodic or sporadic ones.

Boris Sheiko, powerlifting coach

One of the most frequent questions asked of us at my social media agency was 'How much should I post on social media?'. The simple answer is that you should post at a cadence you could keep up for ever, whether that's once a week or once a day.

Cadence is an extension of consistency. It means creating a daily routine that you could do every single day. Creating a life that suits you, that you don't crave a holiday from. Choosing and implementing actions in a sustainable way that means you could maintain the same cadence for long stretches.

Focus and commitment combine with consistency to create small habits that compound. It means a 5 km run twice a week that makes a fitter, healthier you in a month. Writing a blog post a day that leads to your website ranking better in 30 days. An email to your list every week that adds value and builds up their trust and familiarity with your work. A daily cuddle with a family member that leads to your relationship being stronger over time. Reaching out to five new people a day, which means that in a year your network is much, much bigger.

Without cadence we risk peaks and troughs and periods of boom and bust, even when our intention is consistency.

In the cadence game you create the rules of what you will do every week, then keep at it. Create the rules, create the habits, ship when you say you will and keep going. The big breaks, opportunities and exponential growth that follow will look like overnight success. Others won't realize how much you put in, but that won't matter.

Silver bullets

For my book *Instagram Rules* I interviewed the founders of Tentsile, a tree tent and outdoor hammock company that creates tents that can be suspended in mid-air from trees in an environmentally friendly way. Jess from Tentsile explained that the brand 'grew overnight in early 2017 from a viral Facebook video posted by the influencer David Wolfe'. This led to Tentsile's products selling out and the USA becoming its number-one market. 'We couldn't produce fast enough or keep up with retailer enquiries, and since then the #tentsile hashtag has been used over 25,000 times. The brand has harnessed that viral phenomenon ever since.'

It sounds like a fairy-tale story that started with a big break, but that big break came more than two years after the company started an

Instagram account and even longer after the team began developing and creating products. Tentsile posted three times a week from Instagram before David Wolfe made a video about its product. The production lines were set up. The viral post was a result of years of focus, excellence and consistency, of laying groundwork, even when the company didn't know for sure what the future would hold. It trusted it was on to something and, like its tents, it hung in there.

Everyone is looking for a silver bullet because we want the easy way to success. That's the lottery mindset. We want the prince charming or the fairy godmother who's going to save everything. But they're all an illusion.

Carrie Green founded the Female Entrepreneur Association, a membership organization with 6,000 members. She is often asked for her formula for building a successful membership organization by those looking to emulate her success. In truth, Carrie blogged every day and created inspirational videos every week for three years before she even used the word 'membership'. For a long time she didn't have anything her growing network could buy because that wasn't her focus. Her focus was adding value, putting her work out there. Her membership launch was a success because of the extensive groundwork she had laid.

The more work you create, the more of your art you put out to the world, the more chance of something resonating in a huge way. An article, video or product that you weren't sure about could spark someone's imagination and take off. The skill lies in consistently shipping. In creating and publishing, even when you don't feel like it, you turn production into a habit with the power to snowball. 'You can't skip steps,' said Jeff Bezos. 'You have to put one foot in front of the other. Things take time. There are no shortcuts. But you want to do those steps with passion and ferocity.' You have to believe that the rewards are coming.

Spending years sharing how-to videos before launching a membership site isn't sexy, but it's necessary. Creating a solid brand and production lines before approaching influencers isn't sexy, but it's necessary. Over time, focus, excellence and consistency compound. No silver bullets required. In truth, even what looks like a silver bullet rarely is.

Perhaps you're already shipping consistently and a silver-bullet big break really is around the corner. A better strategy, however, is changing your trajectory by a few degrees. Over the longer term, it makes a far bigger impact.

Slow lane

The answer to your Ten Year Career might well come from your existing business, or in something you are already doing. Finding scale where no one else is looking for it can be just as fruitful a strategy as starting a side project or entirely changing course.

Dave Maclean is the CEO of Packt Publishing. Packt commissions authors and creates non-fiction books on technology subjects. The company employs a team of writers, editors and tech specialists. Packt works in partnership with authors to sell their books. By one definition, Packt is a slow-lane business because its main product is content written by humans. Slow-lane businesses scale in a linear way and involve people and products. Fast-lane businesses are those that are exciting, investable and focused on technology. Their growth could be exponential without increasing headcount.

Maclean is a supportive member of the UK's tech community. He mentors founders and will help anyone looking to learn or pitch. He became the first sponsor of my children's book, *Code-It Cody*, and Packt has supported many projects of this nature. One day over lunch I told Dave that my agency would never make me wealthy because it was a slow-lane business that only scaled by headcount. I compared it to a friend's company. He was building a tech platform with the potential to be a fast-lane business.

Dave sighed. He told me that he often met founders who had created platforms that presented content in different ways. Some helped people find or process information faster; others used AI to create graphics and videos from the content. Dave would nod along in interest, asking helpful questions, until the meeting reached the crescendo question: 'Can we use Packt's content on our platform?' The founders had the idea and prototype for the platform, but they hadn't laid the groundwork to make their product viable. Dave's answer? 'Our content is our business; you can't have our content.' His entire business was a content-making machine. Packt had systems and processes geared to working with authors and releasing new titles. They approached authors, accepted pitches, produced books and sold them. Dave helped businesses, but he wouldn't give away his product. The founders inevitably realized that what they had dismissed as a slow-lane business actually held the value theirs was missing.

Life in the slow lane can work out very well as long as you keep going. Think of the tortoise and the hare in business form. By 2019 Packt had published over 6,500 books during 16 years of operation and had a turnover of $30 million. It was the slow-lane business overtaking all the others.

Thinking in terms of fast lane and slow lane or looking for silver bullets over consistency can mean you miss out on the steady upward journey that compounds in favour of the one that might win big. Dismiss nothing.

Ideas

An occupational hazard of entrepreneurship is constantly thinking of new ideas. Ideas for new businesses are dangerous. At best, you start with one and give it all of your focus. At worst, you start a side business that divides your time. A strategy of ideation is valuable, but only if your vetting process is sound.

An ideas strategy that multiplies is where you think of ideas that bolster or progress your business. Ideas for how you make customers happier. How you add more value to your network. Topics to train your team in. Complimentary services to add. Skills to hone. When you focus your ideas energy on your business, you see it in a fresh light.

An ideas strategy that divides is where you think of ideas for other, unrelated businesses or products. Developing and launching these can cost your business in a big way. Adding side projects, adding a disconnected string to your bow or another hat to wear, is a strategy of addition that results in division. Divided use of your time, energy and potential.

In the back of my notebook are all the business ideas I've thought of while on walks or in conversations. Most of them are bad and some are terrible, but I write them into mini business plans. Ideas include the Meaty Muffin Company, for muffin-based savoury convenience food, and a chain of fitness centres called Cinespin, where members turn up and do a spin class together while watching a film. The list includes various concepts for YouTube channels, blog themes and crazy inventions to solve a very specific problem, none of which I'm in danger of creating. (If anyone wants to roll with the two I've described, be my guest!) These are ideas that divide, and while they're fun to think up and write down, I knew I wasn't going to pursue them while I focused on my agency.

If, while growing and systemizing my agency, I had bought domain names and set up landing pages for every new business I dreamed up, it would have cost my Ten Year Career. The notebook was key to making sure the ideas were remembered but not actioned.

The point of my ideas page, therefore, is not to think up my next business idea, launch a product or YouTube channel. It's simply to train my ideas muscle. Consistently coming up with ideas and developing them can be a keystone habit.

You might be one idea away from completely changing your business's trajectory or beginning a game-changing partnership. Your next idea could be how your company secures its biggest client yet, or who to call for help with a challenge. You might be one idea away from a product that becomes your flagship offering or a service that sees customers lining up to do business with you.

My agency was transformed every few years by ideas that we discussed and implemented. The business doubled in size after we won some business awards because we acted on the idea to submit entries as an experiment. Our monthly recurring revenue grew by 20 per cent straight after we introduced Facebook ads management. Half of our clients upped their contracts within the same month as soon as we hired a head of graphic design. I can clearly remember when each idea arrived, the steps we took, and how it made an impact.

Ideas are currency. An idea can be conceived, tested and launched within a few days. You could have a working prototype and a landing page in a week, ready for feedback. You could be running ads and making sales within a fortnight.

Great ideas make an impression. At my agency we would win the clients for whom we had the best ideas. We would do our best work when it came from great ideas. Team members practised becoming ideas machines by thinking up plenty of ideas daily. Our ideas muscles grew, and the practice created an ideas culture in which no idea was too silly. In fact, the sillier the better. Everyone benefitted.

When you become an ideas machine, you'll know the great ones when you see them. Having lots of great ideas doesn't mean you need to run with them – hence the back page of a notebook. Your attention and focus matter too much to be thinly spread. Going in different directions will split energy no matter how much you work.

Make ideas something you have every single day. Train your ideas muscle and become an ideas machine. Ideas plus habits equals success.

Feedback

Shane was an Apple employee whose job was to visit app developers and talk to them about how they could get more downloads. Apple wanted apps to do well in its App Store; these visits were in everyone's best interests.

Shane turned up for meetings and sat down with developers and founders. Having researched the app, he made suggestions for improvements that he knew would make a difference. He was excited to present them. Most meetings went well. Shane's feedback was taken on board and the improvements made. In some meetings, though, he was met with a wall of defence: 'We've already fixed that', 'Our users like that feature', 'Jenny thinks it looks good', 'No, you're using it wrong', 'That's not what our users say', 'That was my idea' ...

The guards went up, and no feedback got through. Shane wasn't going to sit there and fight with people he considered his partners. In these situations he calmly rose from his chair, said, 'Okay, well you clearly don't need my help', picked up his things and walked out the room.

It was a ballsy move – and he never made it out. He was always stopped. An apology came, and the rest of the discussion was open. Shane's bold defiance reminded the app team that they were on the same side.

If everyone around you is reading the same business books and listening to the same podcasts, your valuable insights and useful feedback need to come from somewhere else. If you think the same as everyone else, you'll get what everyone else has and you'll retire in your sixties. If you become brilliant at listening, asking the right people the right questions, being open to hearing their point of view, discerning what will work from what won't and willing to implement the former, your business will always be ahead of the bandwagon.

If your business is an app in the App Store, an Apple representative whose goal is securing you more downloads is someone to listen to. Sorting through their words to find those golden nuggets is a worthwhile endeavour.

Gathering feedback from past and present clients as well as lost prospects is another valuable endeavour. It's never too late to tweak your product, service, website or messaging. The questions could be as simple as 'Why did you buy from us?' or 'Why didn't you buy from us?'. Then there's 'Why did you stop working with us?'. Don't fear asking for feedback because you might hear something you don't like or because you'll have to change something. This is the difference between rapid improvement and the mediocrity that keeps you treading water.

Genuine, helpful feedback from big thinkers is golden. Feedback from people who understand your challenges and want to help is golden, too. Even if you don't take the advice, listening, asking questions in return, and playing around with ways forward might lead to break-throughs.

But feedback and advice are only valuable if carried out in the right way. Every person who reads your article, uses your product or experiences your brand will have a different opinion. That's glorious, because you get to hear a range of opinions that you can decide what to do with. Feedback becomes dangerous when asked of irrelevant people, for example, not the intended audience of the product. There's a phrase, 'A camel is a horse designed by a committee'. Asking too many people for feedback can lead to a product that tries to do everything for everyone.

When asking for feedback on aspects of your business, make some choices. When do you want the feedback? Choose the feedback window and stick to it. If too soon, the concept isn't far enough along for meaningful pointers. Too late and it's, well, too late.

Who will you ask? The perfect people to ask for feedback are thoughtful members of the target audience. Those who will tell you why something should change rather than just say they don't like it. Those who will give helpful comments with direction.

Knowing your audience inside-out, quizzing them about their challenges and fears, and being confident that what you are creating overcomes them, will make it obvious who to ask for feedback. Guessing what another group of people may or may not think often ends up being wrong. Generalizing is hard enough even if you are a member of the audience.

When you want feedback, direct it with specific questions. A UK railway company recently emailed a survey to ask when I would use the train again. The survey was ten multiple-choice questions, with a box at the end for comments. The survey's design meant that thousands of customer completions would have provided useful data. If they had only included the comments box, the feedback would have been reduced to anecdotes.

In the case of the Apple meetings, the app teams that benefitted the most from Shane's feedback were those who had specific questions for Shane. The questions directed his attention to specific places and focused on where they felt they needed the most guidance.

I love the question 'Does it resonate?' because it relates to someone's emotional response to your work and brings insightful answers. Gather insights on the best- and worst-received parts by asking, 'What's the best line, or the best-feature? If we were to only keep one part of this, which should it be?' The same works for the part that isn't understood or required: 'If you had to remove one feature, which would it be? If you had to remove one paragraph, which would it be? Does anything sound slightly off?'

When my co-author and I were ready with the manuscripts for our children's storybooks, we went on a feedback mission. We asked multiple questions of teachers and parents and pored over the answers. Once they had been taken on board and the final manuscripts were produced and printed, we were careful that the line was drawn and communicated. It was no longer, 'Let me know what you think'; it was, 'I hope you love the book.' Or simply, 'It's ready for you now.' Decide when you want the feedback and be open to it. Then make the changes and launch.

Feedback loops

If your consistent efforts aren't bearing the fruits you want them to, work out why. Are you putting in your best work every day? Are you approaching your business with the best version of yourself? Perhaps the market isn't ready for you. Perhaps there isn't demand for what you're supplying. Maybe you're just around the corner from something huge. It's easy to chalk up a slow-moving project or business as a 'slow burner', something that becomes more successful or in demand over a longer period of time, rather than becoming huge straight away. While that can happen, there is also something called slow burner fallacy – a trap you must avoid.

A feedback loop is where you analyse the results of your efforts and use the insights to pivot or redirect your course. Thinking in this way means you don't plough on with a lost cause or fall for slow burner fallacy. Small amounts of progress can amount to big things over time, as long as you keep feeding the fire. Look back over your input and your 30-day challenges to see what worked and what didn't work. Look over your client list or Google Analytics and work out where your new clients are coming from. Be critical of your own journey at every stage, and ensure it's aligned with the goals you have set out.

This story from entrepreneur Daniel Priestley, my co-author on *How to Raise Entrepreneurial Kids*, sums up what can happen when feedback loops aren't in place:

> Today I did a coaching session with an entrepreneur. At the start of the session, I asked about what she wanted to achieve. She gave me an exit number that was a life-changing sum of money. We then looked at her to-do list to get there, and she estimated it would take five to seven years to achieve. I ran through an exact calculation of what it would take to get the exit number – EBITDA [earnings before interest, taxes, depreciation and amortization], due diligence, team size, underlying assets, etc.
>
> When we crunched some numbers, 80 per cent of her to-do list was not going to get her closer to the goal. A lot of the planned budgets weren't going to help either. We cut them out and that went straight to the EBITDA number.
>
> One thing that was quite remarkable was that there was a small niche of clients that were especially profitable. So profitable that these clients made up the bulk of current profit. A little bit of digging and we discovered she only needs another 20 of these clients to hit her target EBITDA number to get her dream exit. She has a list of 380 potential clients who fit the description and we estimate she can win at least one deal per month if it's the key focus.
>
> At the start of the call, she estimated that she was five to seven years away from a big exit. Now it's looking like it's 20 months away. Most business owners I speak to are sitting on a treasure trove of value and are a lot closer to their dreams than they think.

Make a habit of incorporating feedback loops to continue the journey of questioning and ensure you direct your energy in the best way.

Add and subtract strategically

How much of your to-do list is getting you closer to your goal? Are your keystone habits serving you? Look at the trends, crunch the numbers, and get critical of how you're spending your time. When I feel as though I'm not making progress, I use the helicopter technique discussed earlier to take a step back and look at my business objectively. I take a piece of paper and split it into four. At the top of each section I write 'start', 'stop', 'less', 'more' and then write down actions I want to start, stop, do less or more of. It sorts frustration into clarity and means I'm being honest with myself about what needs to change. Adding and subtracting is a great place to start.

Subtract: Actions that aren't contributing to your goals. Arbitrary processes and policies that aren't having the desired effect. Getting involved in routine decisions your team know how to make. Things you do out of obligation instead of desire. Any part of your day-to-day that zaps your energy. Question your habits to remove those that aren't serving you.

Add: More of what's working. Experiments and tests around your processes, in a 30-day challenge, then assess at the end. Committing to meeting a new person every day. Creating a new manual. Following someone up. Publishing something on a specific medium. Improving something.

With consistency and excellence in mind, add and subtract wherever necessary. Another paradox: be flexible with your focus and pliable with your policies. Tend towards excellence in every part of your work.

Advice

If someone tells you their website was expensive, what's the number that pops into your head? £1,000? £5,000? £20,000? £100,000? It's all relative. One person's expensive is another's good value. One person's day off is another's chance to learn. References matter.

Taking advice matters because advice is nuanced. Someone advises based on their references, their image of the world, and their impression of what's possible. They consider your challenge from the viewpoint of their values and preferences for how they spend their time. Do theirs match yours?

Find yourself a millionaire mentor. Listen to people who think big. Find those for whom the default is that they will succeed. Learn how to recognize limiting beliefs or small-minded opinions and don't fall for them yourself. Question the advice you get and be open to every possibility, including respectfully ignoring it. This isn't about dismissing others or having disdain, it's about awareness of your own path and values.

Advice is useful when it stops you making a mistake you would have otherwise made. It's useful when it shows the best way to approach a certain person, a way of structuring something, or a new route to explore. Suggestion-based advice where it's up to you to conduct research and make your decision is invaluable, and people who will nudge you in the right direction without being pushy are worth their weight in gold.

Advice isn't useful when there's information missing. When the advice giver has an agenda they haven't disclosed. When it's based on what worked before, which is unlikely to work again. Or when it's based on what didn't work before, yet could well work again. Along the road of running a successful business there are plenty of tests and plenty of teachers, but there's no mark scheme. The mark scheme is your reasoned judgement and considered choices. No one else's.

At university I had a professor of business psychology who didn't like the idea of profit. And she was teaching a business class! If you don't question the advice you hear, you might not realize someone else's references are becoming yours. Your path might veer off course. The best advice givers are coaches without titles.

Many companies have policies that govern how they operate. They ensure the actions of everyone representing the brand are true to its ethos. As well as deciding when you will and won't ask for feedback, develop a series of personal policies that you stand by.

Developing policies

At my agency, we would receive enquiries for services beyond our core offering. 'Do you do PR?' 'Do you do email marketing?' 'Do you make flyers?' Our policy was that we wouldn't deliver work we weren't sure we could do well. The team knew that our priority was doing great work, not selling our customers any service. Upon talking to our clients we often discovered they wanted something different from what they thought they did, and then we could look after them. If they wanted something we couldn't offer, however, we would say no but help them find a way forward.

Policies give your team members autonomy within standards. They help you get on with your work because they minimize inconsequential questions. Even if you work with freelancers rather than employees, they are working to help you achieve your vision of your company and need to know how it works.

Work out what is standard and non-negotiable and what to take case by case, which is likely less than you think. Businesses that scale make a blueprint for their winning products or services. They sell more of them because their systems can handle it. Most companies do this too late. They do it when they have to; when their investors ask to see documentation or when they start to grow. Make it second nature to write up processes for everything you do or train someone else to do.

Policies equal scale. They create order, solid foundations, and consistency. Create the vision, communicate it, show how it works in practice, invite edits and don't leave success to chance.

Different companies require different policies, but creating rules means you don't take everything case by case. Case by case is how you stay small and get bogged down in detail. Case by case means you become the bottleneck for every decision. Exceptions to policies should be infrequent, made or considered only when something is too curious not to explore further. Even then, approach with caution.

Developing exceptional policies and communicating the why behind them empowers team members to excel. The why matters, because the policy is undermined if it's communicated as 'what management wants', or 'just how we do things here'.

When I worked as a waitress in a South American restaurant, I learned their 'ten key points of service' policy for how waitstaff should engage with customers. Each new team member learned the ten points and received them on a laminated notecard.

The ten key points of service made perfect sense. We were to greet a customer entering the restaurant within a certain number of seconds and seat them within a certain number of minutes. There were stipulations on every part of serving a table well, with timings, including taking drinks and food orders, how long starters and mains should take as well as checkbacks, dessert menus and the bill process.

The why behind the ten key points of service was clear: so customers had the best possible experience, uniform across the chain's servers and restaurants. The consistent service and food developed trust in the brand, and we often served people who were regulars of the chain but restaurant-hopped between cities.

Of every policy, ask two questions: Why, and who's it for?

My agency's policies were written up into a manual. At the time of acquisition, the manual contained 50 sections, each addressing a specific part of the business and explaining why. The policies were open for review and changes could be suggested by any team member, but the benchmark was in place. They created a consistent experience for our clients while empowering our team to do their best work. They reduced the admin that no one wanted to do and took away case-by-case decisions.

Every time you sit down at your computer or begin your work, follow a process that allows for creativity within structure. It's freeing rather than restricting. The same great service plus individual touches. You might use template emails containing key information but personalized to each recipient. There might be a process for a certain task, with opportunities for creativity and flair at specific points. Producing content can also follow this pattern. You might record a video every day in which the format is the same, but you vary the topic or the references. Or a podcast series where you interview different guests within the same structure.

At my agency we had a responsibility manual, developed from my four-column spreadsheet described in Chapter 5, in which I laid out every business process and whose responsibility it was. This wasn't an organizational chart; it was a policy for who looked after every process and who had the final say on what, and why.

There was a pricing policy that included how to price different monthly services, how to work out project pricing, how to handle negotiations as well as helpful sentences to use. There was a brand and style policy that covered our fonts, colours and logo rules. It meant that everything that went out with our brand matched and removed the need for discussion or case-by-case decisions across assets. Our graphic designer knew the standards, so he got on with his role.

The manual sections included email signatures, how to fill in our CRM software and how to create webinars in our webinar software. There were manuals on how to get off to a great start with a client, how to run a successful meeting, as well as social media platform-specific pointers. Each process was mapped out and marginal calls or parts that required decisions came with guidance. There were 'if this, then that' sections to pre-empt anything that might occur. It allowed the team to ramp up output and take complete control of their own areas.

Policies weren't always created in one go; they often developed over time. Our proposal checking policy was a list of pointers to check before sending a proposal to a client. Before the policy existed, the sales team checked proposals for each other and gave feedback by email. After making the draft policy, we added new comments to the document and made rules for what to do in the future. Over time each new proposal was closer to being client-ready. The comprehensive policy saved time, improved proposal quality and gave our sales team more autonomy. Soon the process was inherent, but the policy existed as a backup.

During the execute phase you should collect information and write it down. Notice which questions you answer repeatedly and when your team members most need you. Come up with the rule, communicate it, and make that the default next step for when the question arises next. During your systemize phase, turn these rules into FAQs, processes and policies.

As part of a productive and inclusive culture, it's essential that policies are up for discussion and that every member of your team feels empowered to suggest changes if they see a better way. If the why isn't clear, policies will feel arbitrary or irrelevant. Not questioning and improving processes impedes forward movement just as much as not having them. Remember, we are trying to unlearn the practice of blindly following that schooling instils, not continue it throughout our careers. Own the processes but don't let them own you.

Progressing through the four stages of entrepreneurship and progressing a Ten Year Career requires space to think, zoom out and work on that which only you can do.

Make a policy with yourself for when you are available for your team and clients and when you are not. If your team members ask you questions that they could ask Google, you can't move forward. When running my agency I was either in a different time zone to my team or I had specific 'office hours'. By setting and communicating your restricted availability, your team will have to be resourceful outside of those hours. Being too available creates overreliance on you to provide the answers when your team is probably perfectly capable of working them out.

Make a policy for when you will jump in with the answer and when you will leave others to figure it out. Things you do and don't say. Your personal policies are about boundaries and how you want to work. Once you create them, stick to them and others will too.

Policies aid quality, consistency and cadence, which compound over time to give astounding results.

Making it look easy

The lights flashed, the cameras rolled and the presenter's voice boomed over the speakers. 'And this, ladies and gentlemen, is your winner!'

Hannah confidently strode over to pick up her trophy. With a beaming smile showing rows of perfect white teeth, she waved elegantly to the crowd as they rose to their feet to clap and cheer.

Once backstage, however, Hannah wasn't in the mood for smiles. She kicked off her stilettos, grabbed her pyjamas and started downing water from the bottle someone thrust into her hands. She scrubbed the layers of make-up off her face and peeled off the false eyelashes that had started to itch. She lay on the couch and breathed a sigh, a mix of exhaustion and relief.

In the lead-up to that year's national championships, training had been tough. Being a pro bodybuilder meant 5 am starts, gruelling workouts of every muscle in her body plus weighing out every ounce of food that she ate. The routine had made for a challenging few months as Hannah prepared to compete.

Arriving at the competition venue was just the beginning. As she performed on stage, Hannah was in agony. She was dehydrated in order to look her leanest and felt under pressure to defend her title. Her complex posing routine, perfected through hours of choreography and practice, involved flexing specific muscles and relaxing others, in perfect sync. Her feet hurt from the five-inch stilettos and the bikini dug in to her sides. It was paramount, however, that Hannah smiled, moved and posed with ease and grace. It was paramount that Hannah made it look easy.

Complaining about how hard you're working or the tough time you're going through is rarely a good look, especially on social media. It's always better to have an inner circle, as small as possible, of trusted confidants and use them as your sounding board for tough days. Share the open wounds with them and save the battle scars for the public arena. If I remember that everyone I know is working hard, and everyone I know has tough times, it puts mine into perspective. It means my conversations focus on furthering relationships rather than complaining or being negative.

Everyone works hard. If you're running a business or trying to make a profound difference in the world, you will be working hard. It's a given. And since you're human you have a load of other stuff to deal with: family, friends, taxes. Losses and sorrows and stresses might come and go, but they do for everyone.

In every interaction I have with each person I meet, or every time someone sees my name or face online, I know that I have their attention for a fleeting amount of time. I'm careful that I don't waste it. If I have only five minutes with someone who I bump into on the way somewhere, I want those five minutes to leave each party feeling better than when they started.

Committing to positive encounters has unexpected benefits that you only discover when you do it. *Sprezzatura* is an Italian word that first appears in Baldassare Castiglione's 1528 *The Book of the Courtier*. It's defined as 'a certain nonchalance, so as to conceal all art and make whatever one does or says appear to be without effort and almost without any thought about it'. In *The 48 Laws of Power* by Robert Greene, law number 30 is 'Make it look easy'. Making it look easy can become your superpower.

Candice, whom we met at the beginning of this chapter, had made it look easy. She hadn't grumbled or shared much of the journey. She got on with exercising and making better food choices. When she emerged after summer looking and feeling fantastic, onlookers assumed she had found a silver bullet and they wanted to know what it was.

When she disclosed what she had been doing to the people crowded around her, they found out her 'secret' was actually a lot of effort for a long time. At first, Candice's confession seemed to take away the magic because there was no magic spell. Then the crowd realized it was even more special because of the focus and discipline it must have taken. *Sprezzatura.*

Your career is a chalk line made up of tiny dots of chalk, each one representing a moment in time. A solid foundation, a keystone habit, a good day, a great idea. Chunking these days together creates an upward trajectory. Comprehensive policies, awesome team members and a cadence you could keep up for ever means an unrecognizable life in 30, 60 and 90 days. When you look back in a year's time, you might not recognize your former self.

The next chapter will look at growing, while keeping the endgame in mind.

Key takeaways

- Your Ten Year Career trajectory is made up of thousands of dots. Each one matters.
- Treat your time like the finite resource it is.
- Develop and implement habits to make excellence your default state.
- Curate your focus towards the positive.
- Practise a consistent cadence.
- Don't waste your time seeking silver bullets.
- Exercise your ideas muscle.
- Embrace feedback but think critically when accepting advice.
- Create your policies and make sure your team understands the why behind them.
- *Sprezzatura* – make it look easy.

Less hope, more strategy

Head over to the free *Ten Year Career* companion course for short videos and bonus downloads to apply this chapter's concepts and frameworks to your life and business.

Find it at jodiecook.com/TYC

8

Never Stand Still

• • •

I had come to the end of my first Ten Year Career.

They arrived at 10 pm but I didn't see them until the next morning: the final heads of terms, with the deal we had been looking for and the end-game we had planned. I scanned the email and knew that we were there.

Straightaway it felt like a huge weight had lifted. I felt freedom and possibility. The next few months were a blur of paperwork and checklists, and then it was completion day. The agency I built from my spare room was going on to bigger and better things. The team were being looked after, and it was great for our clients. It was great for me. It marked the end of an era but the opening of a new chapter. I was looking forward to all of our futures.

During the six weeks the deal took to complete, I was awaiting completion while not willing it to hurry up. Being happy in the moment. On purpose, I didn't think too much about the next steps. I knew I wanted to write but hadn't planned what. I knew I wanted to travel but hadn't planned where. I hadn't let myself get caught up in planning the future after sale because I knew I had a deal to do.

We had been snapped up because we were a growing business. The agency had demonstrated growth year on year. The winning bidders weren't buying our current form; they were buying what we could become in the future. The track record and team had proven the agency was capable of more.

In this chapter we're going to talk about growth. We'll cover growing as a business and growing as a person; mastery; accountability; learning; and mentors. We explore the most valuable elements of growth, growing a network and growing a team, and I share the colossal mistake that nearly cost my company. We visit common blockers to growth and how to remove them, including how to push through a plateau. We discover how to find growth opportunities in places no one else is looking and we define the endgame to keep your eyes on the prize.

Mastery

Steve Jobs wasn't a software developer, but that didn't stop him. Plenty of CEOs of tech companies don't know how to code. It's surplus to requirements. They know how to discuss a project with a developer or test the user experience and give feedback. They understand what is possible, so when they find a partner with the right skills, they can build anything they want. If Jobs was busy coding, he wouldn't have been able to fulfil the role of a CEO. Jobs was there to hire the right people, communicate the vision and make sure there was cash to deliver it, not write lines of code.

Before you hire or outsource, however, chances are you will do everything in your business yourself. Entrepreneurs tend to have a good level of knowledge in lots of areas.

Here's why. Imagine a bell curve graph that represents normal distribution for any area of knowledge. At the peak of the curve is the most common level of expertise, around which the majority of people probably sit, hence the bell curve. If you sit too far to the left of the curve's peak on the x-axis, you know comparatively little about the subject. Your only choice is to hire people to explain it and do it. If you sit much further along the x-axis, to the right of the bell curve, you are a master of the subject. Being a master means you focus on what you do best and outsource everything else to the people you hire.

Being just to the right of the peak of multiple bell curves is the sweet spot for entrepreneurs. You hold enough understanding in a subject to know when someone else is a master. You know the difference between good and bad. You can manage a master in the field. This is where entrepreneurs tend to sit on a lot of different subject areas including accountancy, contract law, search engine optimisation (SEO) and Wordpress. Their bell curve position might represent their proficiency for their company's work: you're not an expert copywriter but you know a good headline when you see it. You're not a whizz at Facebook ads but you can talk about strategy and audience and messaging while a master runs the campaigns.

Being proficient in multiple areas is necessary for most entrepreneurs. It can also be dangerous. It makes it tempting to give opinions and block projects rather than moving out of the way and letting your team do their thing.

Knowing your craft inside out and working at it means you become a master. Within your company, what will be your undoubted strength? Some entrepreneurs are fantastic communicators. They build a network and they share their message, driving interest in their company. They are the public face of their brand. Others are master organizers. They can run a company like clockwork and get everyone else on board with their methods. Others have an eye for marketing and know how to position their brand and reach the right people.

In 2017 Gymshark's co-founder Ben Francis stepped away from the CEO role at his firm, which was valued at $1.3 billion in 2020. His passion and area of mastery was marketing. Between 2017 and 2021 Ben was Gymshark's chief brand officer; he chose someone else for the CEO role until the marketing function didn't require his leadership, then he became CEO again when he felt it was the right time.

Self-awareness coupled with a willingness to renounce specific areas to others is how growth happens. While you might never renounce responsibility or ownership of the company, giving others autonomy over certain areas, once trained, leads to growth. You grow yourself by choosing what you want to be good at and known for. You grow yourself by identifying weaknesses and finding those for whom your weakness is their strength. There is no shame in hiring specialists to work alongside and learn from.

The well-known phrase 'jack of all trades, master of none' commonly refers to a wheeler-dealer character. Originally 'jack of all trades' was an admiring term to describe a playwright who helped out in theatres in any way he could. He would help with the stage, the set and the costumes. He would remember lines and try directing. This first person to whom the phrase was applied was none other than William Shakespeare. In modern times a fuller version has developed: 'A jack of all trades is a master of none, but oftentimes better than a master of one.' However it's phrased, it is meant as a compliment.

Being a master of one thing might mean you are an artist or an academic. Being a master of more means your work has a chance of reaching people. You don't wait to be discovered; the power is in your hands. Holding good working knowledge of a lot of areas is desirable. Master of many.

Pick your areas of mastery, and make a plan for the others. Automate, delegate, eliminate. It involves, first, knowing how to become the master of something and doing it, then assessing where your gaps lie – what do you know nothing about that you should know about? – and finally, knowing what you want to train others to do, and knowing where you want to hire other masters.

Accountability

A big factor in my company and personal development was joining an accountability group. It's a group on Telegram in which six of us, working in similar areas, help and support each other. Every Wednesday is Challenge Wednesday, where we share the main challenge we're working through. Sometimes we invite suggestions or questions; sometimes we merely update. Each Friday is Good News Friday, where we share our weekly wins. Each week members will have secured new business opportunities and written more of their books, signed new clients, or worked on areas of their personal development. It's a group of winners, and I love it.

Not only do you become a combination of the five people you spend the most time with, but their standards also become yours. Their references become yours. You become limited by their limitations or set free by the height of their thinking.

Accountability can come in different ways. Perhaps you journal every day and hold yourself to the goals you set. Perhaps you have a mentor or coach who checks your progress against what you say you will do.

Cement great habits by joining a group of people who already hold the habits you want. It makes them seem normal, and you will unconsciously follow suit. Before joining my group, I knew I wanted to think bigger and write more. The group introduced accountability partners who understand my work and I theirs. It creates referrals, expands my mind, and speeds up learning curves because of the willingness of each member to share.

To put together a valuable group, seek out people on a growth trajectory who share your values and who are also working out how to supercharge their way to the top. You might be able to think of a few people, right now, who would be perfect members of your group. There are online networks in every industry whose business model includes small groups of like-minded people. The Female Entrepreneur Association assigns accountability partners to members. Dynamite Circle, for location-independent entrepreneurs, runs mastermind groups and reciprocal mentorship programmes. Growing with people on similar journeys fast-tracks your progress. It ensures your desired behaviour becomes your norm. The advice is useful, and there's a sense of camaraderie which brings more motivation for growth.

Your vibe attracts your tribe. When you become the best version of you, you find others whose values align with yours. You find those travelling a similar path, at various stages, willing to share.

Learning

It's well documented that leaders are readers. Reading the methods, stories and advice from those who have gone before us and succeeded (or failed) can catapult a journey. Never before has it been so easy to hear from those you admire. Almost any living person you can think of is accessible. They will speak on podcasts or in interviews or at events. They might update their social media and give their spin on various topics. With a few taps you can have the words and thoughts of brilliant people in your ear.

Business books give first-hand experience of how someone else overcame the challenges you are going through. They teach tricks and spark ideas. They show new ways of living or thinking and bring a fresh perspective. They stop you going down a rabbit hole of making your own mistakes and learning what to do from scratch. Instead, you can learn from other people's mistakes. You can spot the warning signs they missed and pivot before it's too late. You can test their growth strategies. You can have a direct line to their voice, as an ally or mentor, right in your hands.

Reading too many business books, however, can be a recipe for disaster. Personal development is personal. When you read someone's advice, they project their experience and opinions onto you. Every book is written from a different perspective. If you don't know your own mind, you can easily flit about, wholly adopting the strategy of the last writer you heard from. It's easy to understand why. Someone turning their experience into a book is probably quite pleased with themselves. They are happy and enjoy life. They want their readers to enjoy their own lives just as much. It's still key to question, to observe instead of becoming sidetracked.

Business books vary in terms of the author's ethos and ways of operating. While *The Everything Store* might make you want to set strict seven-point meeting agendas and storm out if someone arrives unprepared, *How to Win Friends and Influence People* inspires you to remember everyone's name and go out of your way to be kind and reasonable.

The 4-Hour Workweek teaches elimination or delegation for freedom over time and a business that runs itself, while *The Magic of Thinking Big* wants you to go big with your plans and put the hours in to match. *The 48 Laws of Power* tells you to conceal your true intentions, but *The Culture Code* wants transparency to be your mission.

Reading every book and implementing each approach into your business means being pulled in different directions. Straddling multiple strategies is no strategy at all. Conflicting objectives and mindsets of writers will confuse you as the reader if you don't make a plan.

How do you read to your heart's content while avoiding the pitfalls of being advised by multiple sources? You know yourself. Before you open any business book or seek solutions from others, get crystal clear on your own values. What do you stand for? What do you want? What is your personal version of success? Ask the difficult questions that require a lengthy ponder. On your final day here, when you're thinking back over your life, what will mark a life well lived? What are you here to give?

Don't look to others for inspiration on the answers. Find them within you and operate from a solid foundation. A deep understanding of who you are is strengthened by reading books. A vague idea leads to shallow imitation. Look to books to inspire and show you new ways of working, not to change your entire belief system.

Read in themes

When you finish a book you love, that resonates with your world, look to expand on the same knowledge. Find others on the same thread or read the books the author referenced. Theme your reading. If you're on a journey of spirituality, start with Gabrielle Bernstein, then Louise Hay, then Dr Wayne Dyer, then move on to Marianne Williamson. Go from mainstream interpretations upwards, finishing with specialist and deeper texts. Keep going further back until you are reading the people who came up with the original concepts.

Themed reading builds deep knowledge and focuses your energy, and you can apply the tactic to reading on every topic. I read *Stuffocation*, then *Minimalism*, then *Essentialism*, then *The One Thing*. Each offered different takes on doing less but doing it better, a theme I wanted to learn about.

The danger of reading too many business books is confusion around which opinions and strategies to internalize and try in your business. That leads to confusion within your team and processes and doesn't serve you as their leader. Reading business books without a clear idea of who you are and what you stand for will build on unstable foundations.

Notice when you're taking on board what you read without questioning or verifying. Read every sentence as someone else's opinion, not a direct instruction. Be aware of the difference between observing another's journey and following their guidance for yours. As we know, the guidance of the author reflects their references and unique view of the world. Closely following their methods will likely lead you to their version of success, which might not match yours. Question whether what you read is relevant to your path. When you are firmly committed to your career and life goals, you can cherry pick the insights you internalize and simply observe the rest.

Learn from history. Learn from social situations. Learn from your accountability partners. Learn from the mistakes you make and the mistakes others made. Learn from observing other leaders and what they do or don't do. Learn from mainstream sources and learn from obscure places.

Mentors of the mind

Many business owners struggle along until they snap. They let small things mount up until it all gets too much, and then they push everything away and break down. In this breakdown they find their breakthrough. They identify the need for a change, and they make it. In this process they might hire a coach to help.

Great coaches will support you into self-sufficiency. They will remind you that you have the answers within you, but that you must ask the right questions. They ask the right questions until you know how to think for yourself. They provide new perspectives and new ways of framing whatever you're working through.

Explaining your goals to your coach from the outset will mean every session is focused on progress towards them. Once your coach knows your goal is to make work a choice within ten years, they will hold you accountable to this goal. Two people's energy channelled into one specific outcome can give it a better chance of succeeding.

While great coaches guide you along your desired path, bad coaches create dependency. They give opinions on what you should do. They become the teacher and the mark scheme that those still on the education conveyor belt need. Instead of useful accountability, they become the person to blame. The coachee outsources ownership, and the coach's methods become their excuse for inaction.

On my graduate scheme we completed an exercise in which we wrote down the names of three people we admired and three people we disliked, then explained why. The answers revealed our values. They revealed the traits we wanted to embody. The exercise showed me so much. The people I put in my 'dislike' column were brash and showy. They prize material possessions and fakery and hype over output. They say controversial things to get attention but have little in the way of foundation. Spin doctors, not artists. Likely to use hacks to grow a following, instead of providing value. Looking for quick wins and one-ups.

The people I wrote down in my 'like' column are, in the words of personal development expert Robin Sharma, 'accomplished within the world but peaceful within themselves'. They are unassuming and quietly confident. They are minimalists rather than materialists and kind to everyone they meet. They put energy into honing their craft and being exceptional, not blowing their own trumpet. They are rarely riled. They let things go. They convey a sense of playfulness and seem to do everything with ease and grace.

Those three people described in my 'like' column are role models to me. When I read their books and listen to their interviews, I get to know how they think and how they solve problems. I learn their frameworks for running teams and doing great work. Their way of operating informs mine.

Upon completing this exercise, I realized that each of these people would be my perfect coach. If I could channel their wisdom, I would effectively be mentored by them, for free, from the comfort of my own mind.

Now, I imagine speaking to those people whenever I'm working through something tricky. I close my eyes and picture myself talking to them about what to do. I imagine the questions they ask and the advice they give. I use their guidance for my journey. I channel the confidence of one mentor before speaking on stage, and the wisdom of another while in an important meeting. I might consider any next step through the eyes of all three before deciding on my path.

Incorporating mastery, accountability and learning into your everyday results in growth. Upping your self-awareness and asking better questions of yourself means knowing for sure the right direction for you. Learning from a range of different sources means having mentors in your ear, to call upon at any time. If you can work out how to do this, anyone can be the mentor in your mind.

If you decide to formally engage a coach, make sure they know what you want to achieve. Use them as a resource, not a crutch. Keep ownership over your actions and avoid depending on them for progress or approval.

Growing a team

Mike Bandar is officially Britain's best boss.

The newspapers wrote it, so it must be true. Along with his business partner James, he committed his company, Turn Partners, to doing things differently. When Mike hires, he doesn't just look for professional credentials, he hires someone with whom he could spend a month in Mexico. Company trips are a key part of Team Turn life.

Believing that a happy team creates happy bosses, and happy customers, Mike has incorporated flexibility and enjoying life into his company's roles. Every February, in a move known as *foffing* (f***ing off for February), they choose a location and spend the month remote-working there. 'We cover the costs, and although we generally go away for the month, staff can come and go for as long as they please.'

Senior developer Luke, who got to explore hidden waterfalls in between conference calls while in India one February, said he couldn't love his job more. 'I fixed a problem at work that was eluding me for months while sitting on a deckchair, listening to the rolling waves, and generally having a great time on holiday.'

Work doesn't have to mean stuffy offices and regimented hours. Work doesn't have to be separate from life. There's more than one way to grow a team.

It's very possible that letting down your guard and encouraging your team to do the same can lead to elevated performance, work satisfaction, team cohesion, and everyone enjoying what they do. Investing in your colleagues in unconventional ways that none of their friends are offered means that as you progress along your Ten Year Career, they are enjoying every step of theirs.

While going on holiday with your entire team might not be for you, the premise is strong. Great teams give the benefit of the doubt, and team members look after each other. Great team members develop reputations for their character based on their actions, not their CV or covering letter, or how well they did in interview. Their reputations are built on how well they do what they say they will do.

Some people hire expecting someone else to solve all their problems, but it's not the way. Hiring doesn't mean looking for genies or fairy godmothers. Hire when you know what you are looking for. Know yourself and hire with awareness.

Most companies are quick to hire and slow to fire when the opposite would work far better. I can trace every bad hire I ever made back to a niggling feeling in the hiring process. A red flag, a glimpse of attitude, something that we overlooked in favour of speed.

When Layla arrived for her interview, she seemed great. She had a friendly smile, a bubbly nature and clearly had done her research. She gave great answers to situational questions, and she knew why she wanted to join my agency. Then I asked a question about her former role, and the floodgates opened. She asked whether I had heard of her former boss, whom she named. When I said I hadn't, she proceeded to slag her off. Layla gave several examples of bad decisions she thought her former employer had made. She explained how unfairly she felt she was treated, and said everyone she used to work with was trying to leave as a result of this lady's actions.

I left the interview feeling sorry for Layla and her unfair past role. In hindsight, I should have seen the warning signs. There are always two sides to every story, and I had only heard one. What did it say about Layla, that she was gossiping during an interview? If they do it with you, they'll do it to you. Was I the next excuse for Layla's stagnant career?

I was in a rush to hire, so I overlooked things I normally wouldn't have. I skipped stages, I didn't vet properly, and I chose hope as my strategy. She had shown me who she was, but I had chosen not to see. I missed the warning signs and hired Layla. It was a big mistake that ended terribly. After a strong start, with Layla getting on well with clients and being a popular member of the team, things began to go downhill and I was slow to act to stop the slide. What started with eye rolls and backhanded comments ended with many once-brilliant team members being pulled into Layla's vortex of negativity. This culminated in an unsalvageable team dynamic that imploded when they left or had to be asked to leave. It was heart-breaking seeing the impact one bad egg could have on such talented people, and the company took a significant step back as a result.

I let bad vibes into my company without realizing the impact they would have.

I should have ended the interview as soon as the drama tales arrived. I should have checked references, and I should have seen the red flags that were waving furiously. Thereafter, I never ignored my gut, skipped a step of our recruitment process, or hired in a rush. I have learned my lesson the hard way, and I know from that experience that rushing is never worth it.

I don't believe anyone is inherently bad, but some people are inherently wrong for your business. There's a difference between feeling as though you could go for a drink with someone and building a company with them. It's possible to wish someone well, even to like them, without offering them a position.

In some organizations, a potential new hire has to meet multiple people for interviews, all of whom need to agree they are right for the company. You might think that such a laborious and lengthy process would put off great candidates, but in fact the opposite is true. The harder it is to get accepted, the more prestigious the role is perceived. Navy SEALs go through the famous Hell Week before being accepted. Some graduate schemes have over seven levels of lengthy assessments. Even at college level, fraternities and sororities often have difficult, drawn-out and sometimes dangerous initiation processes. The tougher the challenge, the bigger reward the role.

Why do organizations do this? After all, it's a lot of work.

Think of your company as a boat. If the boat is sturdy and fit for purpose, it will not sink. The water will not get in, no matter how long the journey or how bumpy the seas. Imagine now that there's someone in your boat with a hammer. They are tap-tap-tapping on the insides of the boat and they keep doing it. No one notices until those tiny taps have turned into a small crack, then a bigger crack. Then the crack is a hole and water is gushing inside. The boat starts to get lower in the water until it's fully submerged.

The standard recruitment process goes like this: Identify need for candidate and write job description. Post job description online and wait for candidates to apply. Sift, sift and sift some more. Interview the best, keep interviewing and hire the best one. Restart this process every time there's a need for someone new. The problem here is that you're only looking during a short window of time that corresponds with your need. You're betting on the right person finding your job description within that window.

The danger of making the wrong hire is real, and a wrong hire turns a small hammer tap into a sinking ship. Having the wrong people on the wrong seats also costs you the great people who you can't now hire because their position is taken. When you're on that plane to a team-wide trip to Mexico, you want to be sure your squad is sound.

What if, instead, you focused on finding the right people first and then creating the jobs for them? My agency's site had a careers page, populated with what we looked for and what someone could expect from working with us. It had paragraphs from team members about our culture, and it described every part of the selection process. We were transparent about the company and our roles, and we even wrote a section about how someone might impress us. People with whom that page resonated joined our careers list to hear about opportunities whenever they arose.

The form they completed to join the list included space for someone to tell us what they could bring to the role. Great candidates didn't waste this space. We had all sorts of brilliant submissions, and we looked at them regularly. If we suspected someone might be awesome, we didn't wait for a role to become available. We contacted them and started getting to know them. We created roles for some of them and, confident in the agency's growth, we hired ahead of needing to.

This hiring process put the power in our hands. Rather than being backed into a corner or desperate to hire, we were indifferent, with a relaxed openness to being persuaded by the right candidate.

Avoid rushing into hiring decisions by being open to working with brilliant people all the time. It's amazing how everything can slot into place when you have confidence in who is coming on board.

Recruiting bias

There are countless forms of bias that take place during a recruitment process. *First impression bias* happens when recruiters decide whether they will hire a candidate within the first ten seconds and spend the rest of the interview gathering evidence to support their decision. While this has merit, because your clients likely will have a similar impression, it can be limiting. Plenty of people are nervous during the first ten seconds and then settle in. Plenty of people start well and then don't sustain it.

There's the *like me* bias, also called *similarity attraction* or *affinity bias*, where interviewers are drawn to candidates who remind them of themselves. This means that whoever is in charge of hiring will unconsciously create a team of people similar to them. If the original is worth copying, this isn't necessarily bad. However, diversity of thought comes from diversity of people. Variance over clones. Having new perspectives and experiences is more beneficial than everyone looking and thinking the same. While building a team of like-minded people has its advantages, it can mean missing knowledge and opportunities outside your collective sphere.

Other biases include *overconfidence bias*, when a recruiter is so confident in their ability to pick a good candidate that their confidence clouds their judgement; *beauty bias*, where we want to pick the most physically attractive candidate; and *conformity bias*, where our hiring decisions are swayed by what other panel members think.

Avoiding bias in the interview process involves ensuring each candidate goes through the same procedure and is marked in a similar way. It means keeping a log of the questions you will ask everyone. Incorporating stages where you make assessments without knowing someone's name or what they look like. Saving template messages for every part of the selection process. Staying open-minded with everyone you meet rather than making your decision straight away. Then writing up the answers, having discussions where every opinion is considered, and never ignoring those niggling feelings. If something doesn't stack up now, it will become your problem in the future.

The first person I hired was Jason, who would become a social media manager. It was the first time I had been the other side of the table. I was more nervous than Jason, but I didn't let on. I made sure I was sharp with my questions and critical with my thinking. These candidates in front of me, what will they be like to work with? Will my clients like them? Will they be open to learning and will they want to excel? Will it work out? The leap was terrifying but necessary.

Jason's first week came with new tasks including employment contracts, holiday allowances and payroll. When training Jason to follow my methods in looking after clients, I wanted to strike the right balance between supportive and empowering. I didn't want to oversee every detail, but I also didn't want to throw him so far into the deep end that he drowned.

A month into working with Jason I got a call from one of our clients, a comedian we were representing with an act called 'Boris Nicoli, X-KGB mindreader'. We were promoting him during his time at that year's Edinburgh Fringe Festival. 'I need to talk to you about Jason.' Oh no. 'Is everything okay?' I asked nervously. 'Absolutely! In fact, it's more than okay. He's written some tweets for me that are so funny, I want to use them in my show! I wanted to ask if that would be fine with you.'

Even now, that conversation stands out. I remember that feeling as if it was yesterday. Proud and relieved. Excited for the future with a confidence in how it would turn out. I responded, 'Amazing', and skipped across the room to tell my first employee what he'd created.

When hiring and working with people I learned that the relationship was better when I was on a level with that person. Where we worked as teammates, not in a hierarchy. I was looking for leaders: leaders without titles, to own their work. I didn't want to run a dictatorship or be cracking a whip and giving orders. Teams with horizontal relationships give praise between all levels of role or, instead, express gratitude or encouragement and avoid praise all together. Strong teams thrive when horizontal relationships are most prominent. Giving praise implies the passing of judgement by a person of ability on a person of lesser ability, leading to 'vertical relationships' and feelings of inferiority. Phrases such as 'well done' or 'good job', in a work or family context, are likely to only flow in one direction.

After I read about this approach in *The Courage to Be Disliked*, by Ichiro Kishimi and Fumitake Koga, it became my policy. My go-to phrases would be those of gratitude. I would thank my team members for their contribution and tell them how much difference it made. While leadership books told me that praise is key in order for people to feel valued, language based on rewards and rebuking didn't feel right. It felt as though it was creating dependencies, so I switched my method to one based on Kishimi and Koga's teachings. I was amazed when my team members started doing the same in return. They would thank me for how I'd supported them. We ended each Friday by saying thanks to each other for specific instances in the week. The thanks flowed between people regardless of any seniority their job title implied. Adopting this way of working with my team meant our workplace was a fun place to be and our business kept on growing.

Changing your game

It is tough to make predictions, especially about the future.
Yogi Berra, baseball catcher, coach and philosopher

When you're on top of your game, it might be time to change it.

In Chapter 2 we covered seeing the future and what's happens if you don't. Blockbuster should have pioneered Netflix, UPS should have invented Amazon, a taxi firm should have invented Uber. They didn't. Success and complacency often crop up as a pair.

Huge platforms are being invented by outliers – those with the curiosity and expansiveness of mind who take action in the right direction. There are countless examples of businesses that were best placed to invent the future missing it because they were too busy doing what they had always done. They overlooked the opportunities and became obsolete. Industries change and new players emerge all the time.

The sigmoid curve is a mathematical function used to model the natural life cycle of many things, from biological organisms to businesses. It is likely to appear again and again in your life and business. When you hire a team, you form, you grow together, then cracks start to show. When you work with a client, you sign them up, you make initial improvements, then you work harder to achieve marginal gains. When you begin running half-marathons you cut minutes off your time very easily at first, then PBs require a new approach.

In business the sigmoid curve has three stages:

- **Learning.** Akin to the start-up phase of a business, when life might seem like a lot of work with little to show for it, the learning stage of the curve is where the seeds are sown. It's the long days and the endless planning. Input after input, all to move the needle. The learning stage is where many careers and businesses fail, because not everyone has the conviction to push through to stage 2.

- **Growth.** This is where the magic happens. The fruits of your labour start to emerge, and you feel as though you're on top of the world. Opportunities appear from nowhere, revenues increase, good things seem to come at you and don't slow down. Every day brings new joy, a surprise or win. You're unstoppable.

- **Decline.** The final stage in the curve happens when the peak is reached and the downward trend begins. Perhaps revenues plateau and then start to shrink, or a team working well together starts to show cracks. The success that reached new heights is trending downwards.

The sigmoid curve's cyclical nature means that you can never settle. Even when you're on top of the world, be thinking ahead. Don't rest on your laurels. Pre-empt the decline and work to redirect its course.

The worst businesses cling to the growth stage and make cases for doing so. Upon entering stage 3, they hark back to the good old days and want them to return. The best businesses aren't afraid to start from the bottom again, with the confidence that they've done it before. They surf the curve and they're in control. This is their jam.

Michelin was at the top of its game at the beginning of the twentieth century in the tyre industry when it considered the question 'How do we sell more tyres?'. Rather than following a typical approach of more aggressive marketing or advertising, the company tried something different. We will sell more tyres, it concluded, when people drive more – so let's get them to drive more. It invented the *Michelin Guide* for hospitality, first introduced as *The Red Guide* in 1900. At the time, both cars and food tourism were novel luxuries. *The Red Guide* included information about the top-quality hotels and restaurants across France that Michelin believed readers should visit, as well as filling stations and helpful information about how to change a tyre. Michelin produced 35,000 copies of the first guide and distributed them across France.

In 1926 Michelin began handing out stars to restaurants, with one star meaning a restaurant was very good in its category, two meaning it was worth a detour, and three stars meaning it was worth a special trip. Today the *Michelin Guide* lists over 8,000 restaurants and is a key part of Michelin's operations. And it did sell more tyres.

In 2021 Michelin made $24.82 billion of tyre-related revenue, more than Continental and Goodyear put together and second only to Bridgestone with $27.49 billion.

Michelin's execution phase included signing dealers, improving its tyres and marketing to drivers. Its processes were in place, and it was ready to scale. Predicting the future of tourism and making the unconventional *Michelin Guide* move was the result of the scrutinizing that came next.

In a more modern example, presenting coach Rob Geraghty and his team travelled the world before the pandemic, teaching blue-chip execs effective presenting skills. Only a small part of his work was online, but Rob had noticed bad habits creeping into Zoom calls and had some ideas for new training he could deliver.

When the UK's first lockdown began, Rob took that as a sign to adapt. He sprang into action. He renamed his company Presenting

Virtually and started sharing tips in short videos on LinkedIn. He sent one per day for over 100 days, including at weekends, and drummed up interest in what he was doing. In the meantime, he let his clients know that lockdowns didn't have to stop their pitches and meetings from being effective.

Rob's new training explored video chat etiquette, including hosting and participating; technical precautions; and how his clients could set up attractive 'Zoom zones'. The company went from losing all its corporate bookings in one fell swoop to growing by 300 per cent in 2020 compared with 2019. Rob had seen the future and was ready to grow. Rather than lament the business he had lost during the pandemic, he used the opportunity to grow faster.

Look ahead

Take any part of your business and project it forward – one single element, one of the processes it carries out. How will it be done in the future? How will human behaviour change? How will technology change? Businesses that do this critically and regularly are best placed to adapt to anything and spot opportunities for growth.

Consider taking a taxi. Just because Uber changed that process doesn't mean it won't change again. At one point, taxis could only be flagged down in the street. Then they could be ordered by telephone or text or booked in advance. Taxi drivers were hired by taxi companies who did all the booking, and the networks communicated via radio. Passengers paid by cash at the end of the journey.

Uber onboards drivers, who aren't necessarily taxi drivers, trains and assesses them, and gives them access to an app to connect with passengers. Passengers download the app, request a driver and a driver arrives. The app finds their location, their driver's location, and takes payment by credit card based on mileage and wait time. Uber takes a cut and pays the driver.

When Uber came along, it became a broker for drivers and passengers and it used GPS and the internet. The technology for Uber already existed; the company repurposed it.

In the future, the process will change again. In the future your taxi needs might be synced with your phone or the device that's connected directly to your brain. Your calendar will show where you need to be and by when, your GPS will show your location, and a car will turn up exactly when you need it. Only it might not be a car as we know it. And it likely won't have a driver; it will be autonomous. There won't be a driver to check your face against your picture and confirm it's you, but there might be fingerprint tracking or eyeball scanners.

If that's where the future could take the simple act of travelling by taxi, what about the ancillary processes? Perhaps there will be depots where robotic devices clean self-driving vehicles. What about safety and security? What will happen to car dealerships? Will anyone own their own car? Will we need to travel at all, or will we be plugged into the matrix and living virtual realities? Travel could decrease to zero, and our friend Rob might be busy teaching his clients how to present virtually long after cars no longer exist. What will that mean for human behaviour and purchasing decisions? What will that mean for the planet? Questions lead to more questions, and this game can be played for hours. And they train your brain.

Growing a business is a fun rollercoaster, and whatever plan you decide upon now won't stay the same.

Every ten years or so, something happens that shakes things up. It's likely to keep happening. Seeing the future stops your business becoming irrelevant. Even if you turn out to be wrong, which you most likely will, this practice keeps you ready to capitalize. Markets expand and contract. Sigmoid curves are in action across nature and business. Growth comes to those who predict the future and roll with it, not those who keep their head bowed in denial or fight it.

Life is simple and people make it complicated

As you start to walk on the way, the way appears.

Rumi, poet

At a Prince's Trust event I sat on a panel with four other entrepreneurs. The audience asked questions about starting up, hiring a team, inspiration and marketing, which we took turns to answer. One woman raised her hand to ask her question, and the floodgates opened. She had questions about registering a business. She was concerned about using her home address. She didn't know whether to get an accountant, and she didn't want to be fined for not submitting any documents on time. She wasn't sure if she should get up earlier or go to bed later, but she knew she would need to work more if she was going to make her business a success. As her questions rolled out in a stream of worry, I realized that this woman represented the fear that can take over if we let it.

Rather than answer each of the specific admin questions one by one, I picked up my mic and said, 'I know you have a great business inside you. If you're this diligent even before setting up, you'll soon have clients who love you because you think of everything. But let me tell you this: none of those things you've mentioned should be a blocker to starting. None of them. You will figure everything out.'

She looked more relaxed, so I carried on. 'You can register a business in ten minutes, there are plenty of ways of not using your home address. There are a ton of places to find accountants who will make sure you avoid fines, and it doesn't matter when you do your work. You will find the answer to every one of those questions once you begin, but please don't let searching for them stop you from moving forward.'

Business is simple and people make it complicated. It's not forms or admin or external factors that complicate the way; it's people and their own worries. Once you commit to moving forward, the answers to the inconsequential details will find you. The woman at the Prince's Trust event was worried, but at least she put her hand up. Imagine all the people with the same questions who don't raise their hand. They don't walk on the way, so the way never appears.

When I was young, I loved the Roald Dahl book *Matilda*, about a young girl with family troubles who loves reading. Matilda is never scared to ask questions because she believes she can always learn. I channelled Matilda's questioning ethos every time I asked a question. There are no silly questions.

People make life and business complicated because they think they know what other people are thinking. They fabricate contexts and assume they know how someone else will feel. The result of this storytelling is salespeople who don't call prospects 'because they might be busy' or someone who doesn't make a bold move 'because of what people might think'. But think about it: if someone is busy, they won't pick up.

Those people whose opinions you fear are probably not thinking about you at all. And if they are, so what?

Those voices in your head, putting blockers on progress, are nothing more than the sound of fear. Listening to it stifles growth and makes the simple complicated.

Until we subscribed to a telephone answering service, my agency's phone would ring every hour. Each call followed the same pattern. The caller would open with a concern: 'If you don't have this type of insurance, you'll be in trouble', 'You need a licence for that, otherwise you could receive a fine', 'What would happen if your computers stopped working?', 'Are you protected in case of a GDPR breach?' They would get us scared about something only to offer to sell us the solution.

Every call was irrelevant to what we were there to do, which was to look after our customers. We knew we had everything needed to run a business, so we didn't need to worry. 'Everything should be made as simple and as few as possible,' said Einstein. Even so, after hearing the fear story, someone in the team would Google what they were talking about. Fear is contagious.

Business is complicated when you avoid the big questions in favour of the little ones. The big questions: what will make my business grow and how will I make that happen? The little questions concern admin, inconsequential purchases, anything that doesn't benefit your customers or team. How you should spend your time is easy to know once you answer the big questions. You don't have a nine to five. Your time isn't there to book; it's there to maximize. Blank space in your calendar doesn't mean you can fill it with whatever. It doesn't mean anyone can slot in. It means space to think up ideas and work on improving and endless possibility. Your energy flows where your attention goes. When you focus your attention, it's simple.

Bottlenecks

Before we had received the final heads of terms for the agency's sale, we were in a negotiation process. The other offers I received came with earnouts – periods of time after sale during which the owner continues to work in the business. One potential buyer I loved hadn't understood how my business worked; they wanted me to work in it for a further three years. The key processes were all carried out without me, so that idea made no sense.

The first offer from the company that bought us contained an earn-out of 18 months. A proportion of the sale price was in cash and equity dependent on certain sales targets. I saw a problem, and I got them on the phone. I explained that if I had to stay and work in sales for 18 months to realize the full value of my agency, I would do that. But, and it was a big but, it would stifle the growth of the company. 'How so?' they asked. 'Because', I continued, 'I removed myself from the sales process over three years ago. The salespeople are autonomous. The company has grown year on year because of them, not me. If I have to guarantee certain figures to secure this valuation, I will, but it will mess up the structure and I'll become a bottleneck again.'

They heard me. They understood. The final offer was for the full amount with no earnout, and I would hold a small number of shares in the group company. I was removed as a bottleneck to every part of the agency, and it was ready for more.

After I completed the execute phase of my business at the end of 2014, it was time to systemize. I had to make rules and processes and remove myself as a bottleneck to growth. While I had been executing like crazy, a pile had been building. On the pile were things I needed to approve, decisions I needed to make, people I ought to respond to. My important things got done, but my team members' important things were stuck with me, and that was a problem. I concluded that my job was no longer simply to do my job, it was to work out what to do next. Freeing myself of daily responsibilities was how I would become surplus to requirements and grow the company.

After writing the list of every process that happened within my business, I thought about who to hire – which processes I would get help with. Then I hired and trained people to do them. After that, I switched my first response to every question. Instead of answering directly, I started to use the phrase 'What do you think?'. I knew the person in front of me had the answer inside them, but they were relying on me to tell them instead of getting to it. Many times, on being asked 'What do you think?', they had the perfect answer. I'd say, 'Sounds great', and they'd be off. I replicated the coaching I'd received on my graduate scheme to empower my team to have autonomy.

The most impactful of roles I hired for was filled by David, a social media trainer, who ran group and individual social media training sessions for our clients. He visited the client at their premises or welcomed them into our meeting pod. He won clients over with his knowledge, amusing anecdotes and genuine curiosity for their business.

The first few times that David went off to run a training session, I was afraid. Before he arrived, I had run every training session myself. My lizard brain wanted to get involved. It tried to convince me I was missing something and put the fear in my head that something would go wrong. Nothing went wrong. David knew his stuff and had great ideas. He took on board everything I suggested. Many training clients started booking regularly and became great referral partners or social media management clients for specific services.

While I had been hosting training sessions and doing the follow-ups myself, I was doing a million other things, too. Delivery of training sessions was something I had to squeeze around everything else, but training was David's sole focus. He was a breath of fresh air for me and the company, and his role meant I could make another key hire, sales support. The agency more than doubled in size that year, and both the training and sales departments performed better without me.

After every leap of faith, at times when I was afraid to hire someone new or let go of something, amazing things happened. I removed myself as a bottleneck, and people and processes flourished. I worked hard to delegate to my new team members but not abdicate completely. They kept me informed, and they knew when to ask for support, but they were conscientious people who took pride in owning their roles. Hiring left me with more space to systemize and grow while being completely confident in our offering.

It's impossible to take those leaps with a mindset of scarcity – to not hire because of what might be around the corner. We hired account managers before we needed them, and the work for them always appeared. I liked playing what I called the 'unlimited game'. Imagine you have unlimited time, unlimited cash, unlimited human resource. What would you do, what would you buy, what would you create? The answers inform your next move, and the answers bring about growth.

I had mistakenly thought that there were aspects of my business that only I could do. So much so, I overlooked getting help. I had overlooked passing them to others to see what they could do. Writing down everything that I believed only I could do, then sense-checking it, allowed me to teach others to deliver to the same standards and beyond. I was lucky to find conscientious people with oodles of integrity and a commitment to being exceptional. That behaviour became the norm. I started doing only those things that I could do, and everything else was distributed and shared.

Selling my business had the same effect, but for my entire team. I removed myself as their ceiling to growth. I was honest: the business had grown as much as I had the inclination to grow it. I knew my burning desire wasn't to run a massive agency, but my team was capable of it and wanted to. Removing myself as the owner and passing the baton to someone with bigger agency dreams took away another bottleneck to growth.

When I hired salespeople, I did so to remove myself as a bottleneck to the sales process. When I went away, I did so to remove myself as a bottleneck to resourcefulness. When I sold the company, I did so to remove myself as a ceiling. I was taking advice I had heard from Gymshark's Paul Richardson, who had advised its founders from the company's early days: hire great people and get out of their way.

Other people will want you to fill the roles they have in mind for you. Questions will pull you back in, the precedent set by others will try to dictate yours. But with a clear goal of what you want and what will work, alongside the energy to make it happen, you can achieve any outcome. Industry standards for marketing agency earnouts are anything between 12 months and five years. My transition took two weeks. Make robust processes, hire great people and get out of their way. Train and trust. Delegate without abdicating. Make yourself surplus to requirements, and don't be a bottleneck to any growth.

Saying yes and saying no

Within each stage of a Ten Year Career's journey – execute, systemize, scrutinize, exit – and its corresponding focus comes a daily choice: yes or no. Each day you will receive requests and invitations. Events you could attend. Projects you could start. Distractions you could entertain. Someone asking for your opinion, to pick your brain or get you involved on their journey. Without a solid policy for when to say yes and when to say no, you will fulfil obligations without a sense of purpose. It might feel exciting at first. Then it will feel draining and shallow.

We visited policies in the previous chapter, but your policy for yes and no should be clear at each stage of your business. During one early year of running my agency I said yes to everything, short of being in two places at once. It was a one-year experiment. I gave talks, I sat on panels, gave webinars, held Q&As about topics in my industry and went to every event. I had one-to-ones and let people pick my brain to their heart's content. I said yes, especially to any invitation where I could address a whole room, the pinnacle of invitations at the time. I didn't consider balance; I gave away my time and then assessed where I was.

When I said yes, it was a true yes. I didn't cancel or let people down. I turned up early and I stayed present. I remember looking around events and seeing people sitting in the corner on their phones. There was no point being there in body and not in mind. I immersed myself in each invitation, aware that the next person I met could be my next client or referrer or friend.

My policy at events was to be relaxed. To have open body language, be easy to talk to and have nothing to prove. To be interested in people. I would ask about someone before they asked about me. I would approach people and introduce myself. Not everyone has the confidence to say hi first, but once you get chatting you never remember who approached whom. I would be the solid guest, the great speaker, the one who brought the happy vibes and left the event in a better place.

Saying yes opens opportunities because you never know what's behind those yesses. You can't fathom what might happen, whom you might meet and where it might lead because it's an unknown. People who don't say yes enough, especially in the first stage, might decline invitations because of fear. They second-guess what an opportunity might be like, and they make excuses for why it won't be worth their while. Their lizard brain is trying to keep them snuggled up on the sofa, and they mistake that feeling for intuition.

Saying yes is powerful as part of an intentional strategy. But saying yes to someone else's plans by default means saying no to your own. You can only spend the time once, then it's gone. When you say yes, do it because the opportunity aligns with your goals and your path, not from a place of obligation – because someone has twisted your arm into agreeing. Protect your time and your headspace and save room for the yesses that you really want to do. Above all, say no to everything that reduces your autonomy.

The buyers of my agency created a framework for the agencies they would acquire. They agreed their criteria for saying yes. When meeting potential candidates for purchase, sometimes two per week, they knew what marked a yes and made no exceptions. It wasn't personal or mean, it was a policy. They had fixed resources for acquisitions and didn't want to waste time pursuing deals that wouldn't work. You'll need a policy too.

Saying no can feel mean. That person only wants an hour of your time; surely you can spare it. That talk won't take too long to put together. It's only a quick meeting, promise. Saying no can feel as if you're being rude or rejecting someone. Sometimes the yes is easier.

Weigh up what you would rather have. The short-term discomfort of turning down an invitation you're not super-excited about, or the sinking feeling in your tummy when you realize the invitation you reluctantly accepted three months ago is tomorrow.

I recommend creating an email template for saying no. I also recommend a 'now' page (a concept invented by Derek Sivers). Both guard your time so you can spend it doing what you know will make the difference in your current stage. My now page, at jodiecook.com/now, is up to date with what I'm working on. Sometimes it states what I'm saying yes and no to at that time. Make one and link it wherever people get in touch. It sparks conversation about your areas of focus and gives you an easy way of saying no.

The 'no' email signature goes like this: 'Thanks so much for your email and for the invitation. I'm sorry I'm not able to [nature of request]. Right now I'm focused on one thing and I'm persevering until it's done.' You could add that in the future you might be looking to do whatever they're asking, or see if there's another way you could add value. Everyone's 'no' template will look different, so make one that feels right to you. At some point, it might be a bad use of your time to respond at all.

It wasn't only requests and invitations I started saying no to, it was people who wanted previous versions of me. It might have been the client who wanted me to be their account manager. Or the client who thought I would be on every call. At first, I felt guilty and I'd make exceptions. Then I realized the lack of boundaries was creating the same bottlenecks I had worked so hard to remove. I didn't put my own boundaries in place, so my time, energy and headspace were up for grabs to anyone that asked.

I like to think of it as upgrading. I'm never a finished product; I'm always upgrading. I can upgrade former operating systems of myself and not feel bad about it.

After gaining perspective I could introduce my colleagues and know that they would look after clients. My team members were there to say yes to these requests, and they welcomed them. I stopped operating based on fear. Making sure my team knew the why meant they took pride in protecting my boundaries. They took pride in looking after my former responsibilities better than I once had. They would ask for the guidance they needed and then roll with it.

Bring maths to your 'no'

When considering saying no, think of scale. Your message can resonate with bigger rooms because the rooms don't need to be physical. Millions of people can hear any podcast or webinar. If you record an hour's podcast that has 10,000 listens, you've cloned yourself by a multiple of 10,000. Maths forms part of the yes-and-no equation because the right yesses can take you further and what might have once been a no could now be a yes.

When should you turn acceptances into polite declines? When you reach a tipping point. You might be there already. As soon as you know what you can achieve in one day, whether working alone or with your team, you know the cost of saying yes. When you're somewhere but your mind is somewhere else. When you're searching for more time. When you're as productive as possible but there's too much in your diary.

When you say yes to something that should be a no, you're actually saying no to something that could be a yes, by default. Your time on earth is finite. Far better to have the blank space than a sea of mediocre commitments that you're not excited about and won't make a difference.

Say yes until you can say no, then say no to nearly everything. Say yes until the costs outweigh the benefits. Keep saying yes until you're sure that's the case. Give your all, test your limits of being busy, then create your policy and scale back. Spend your energy on only the opportunities you'd give anything to do and the people you'd give anything to see.

It's lonely at the top

Make no little plans. They have no power to stir man's blood and probably themselves will not be realized.
Daniel Burnham, architect of the Chicago World's Fair of 1893

In 2013 my husband, Ben, and I co-produced a series of children's storybooks that introduce entrepreneurial role models to six- to nine-year-olds. They provide role models that kids might not otherwise meet and are a tool for social mobility. We wanted to introduce kids to exciting protagonists, inspiring confidence, creativity and resourcefulness.

The *Clever Tykes* storybooks sold on Amazon and in stores including Harrods and Selfridges. Seeing them on the shelves of these stores was awesome, but something didn't feel right. Distribution was skewed. They were available in prestigious places, but this wouldn't help us reach those for whom they would make the most difference.

We hatched a plan to find sponsors to donate the books to primary schools. Ben met with corporate social responsibility representatives of banks, looking for small amounts of sponsorship from each branch to sponsor its nearest schools. We planned to secure enough of these sponsorships to cover the whole of the UK – 24,000 primary schools.

A month later a bank agreed to run a pilot of the scheme with five primary schools. The books were printed with the bank's logo on the back and an accompanying letter. Entrepreneurial education sessions that Ben had planned ran in each school.

As we signed and delivered this deal, we weighed up how much Ben had put into it. The total was huge: four meetings, a proposal and lots of paperwork to get it signed. Then there was printing and sending the books, agreeing the wording of the letter and organizing the sessions with schools. As a result of this work, only five schools of 24,000 would receive our books.

At the rate of five or ten schools sponsored per go, we'd need between 2,400 and 4,800 local sponsorship deals. That was untenable. We decided that going big was the only option. A new plan arrived: find one sponsor. One sponsor to gift our storybooks and resources to all 24,000 UK primary schools. Compiling that plan and writing it down made it sound more doable, not less. Before, we were looking for a specific person with a specific title in every single town. Now, we were looking for just one person with the power to say yes, and we knew it was only a matter of time before we found them.

Our strategy was to meet people and tell them about what we were doing and what we were looking for. We didn't meet them to sell to them, just to get on their radar. We told our mailing list. I mentioned the mission in talks. We aligned our energy into one goal: finding the sponsor. Ben wrote to Members of Parliament and bank CEOs and the CEOs of airlines and supermarkets. We weren't asking for them to be the sponsor; we were asking them to keep us in mind.

The new offering was for 24,000 primary schools to receive a set of *Clever Tykes* storybooks. They would also have unrestricted access to the books and accompanying teaching resources via an online portal containing chapter walkthroughs, exercises, lesson plans and a space for schools to book an entrepreneurial education session from a trained volunteer. Everything would be free for primary schools, and parents would be invited to use the portal, too. It would be fantastic.

I visualized hearing the yes. I visualized talking the sponsor through the plan and the timescales and them nodding along. I visualized what the books would look like in print and the reaction of the schools receiving them. I visualized seeing 1,000 schools using the portal, then 2,000 and more. In my head, it all had happened. Now I needed to step into the version of myself that could make this happen, and Ben had to do the same. We had to trust that the daily steps we were taking to spread the message would result in the perfect sponsor saying yes.

It worked. Meeting Sophie led to meeting Henry. Meeting Henry led to meeting Craig. Craig bumped into Martin, who explained that his role was to find projects that fulfilled the mission of the bank he worked for. Craig suggested that Martin meet us and passed on our details. When Martin arrived to talk about the project, he had already started thinking about the logistics of posting the books to every primary school. The stars had aligned and conversations had filtered out and reached him. Our remarkable plan had sparked interest, and Martin was the man who said yes.

Twenty-four thousand schools received our storybooks and resources. A thousand started using the portal in the first week. The impact was huge. Our books made the difference we planned, and to this day we receive messages from schools that use the books in lessons.

Martin told us he received requests all the time, but most of them were for sponsorship of between £2,000 and £5,000. There weren't many that came his way looking for £200,000–500,000. Those that were likely to make a huge impact caught his attention. He liked the audacity. He bought into the vision.

Dreaming bigger captures the imagination. Dreaming small and missing achieves nothing. Big plans have the power to amass a tribe and gather support. We needed to think a hundred times bigger to achieve something with over a thousand times more impact. We needed to not look for a blueprint or a mark scheme because it didn't exist.

It's lonely at the top because there are only a few people there. There are only a few people who realize where the top is. The rest have imagined a ceiling that is actually about 40 per cent of the way up. Most people don't believe they will be able to stop working until they are in their sixties, so they don't imagine a reality where it happens sooner. They take their career goals and spread them over decades instead of thinking about how they can achieve much more in a much shorter space of time.

Because it's lonely at the top, there is less competition. Applicants for entry-level roles outnumber applicants for high-level roles by hundreds. Plenty of those applying for the former could have secured the latter if they had only dreamed bigger. Playing small is easy and comfortable and is what everyone does by default, but it won't change anyone's life. On your journey to the big plans, you'll hit the smaller ones. Make them your fallback, not your plan A.

The big opportunities go to the people who have the audacity to ask for them. Asking for the investment, asking for the opportunity, or asking for the sale. Not just asking and hoping but mapping it out and making a plan. Being happy to know that no one has done it before, but they could be first.

If Ben and I hadn't stopped to make a bigger plan, we'd still be signing small contracts right now. A change in thinking, by a magnitude of a thousand, was required to change the outcome. When there is method in your madness and determination in your eyes, it's catching. It's remarkable and the message spreads, leading to those yesses. Find the top and set up camp.

Endgame

When I received the final heads of terms for the agency's sale, nothing in it came as a surprise. I had visualized it. I had written a pretend cheque to myself for the exact amount of money on offer. I had pictured the heads of terms in my mind and written the press release. I had imagined the conversation about what would be required of me. I had even written the journal entry that my future self would write. It was all happening exactly as it was meant to.

A year before that point, however, it had been a different story. I had an endgame in mind but had done approximately zero to make it happen. In the past we had received offers of purchase, so I thought that more would magically arrive as soon as I was ready. I was wrong.

Every time I walked down the same stretch of road near my house, I had the same thought: I want to sell my agency. (We know that humans have the same thoughts day after day, right?) Once, when travelling this path having the same thought, it hit me. I wasn't practising what I preached. I had intentions and grandiose plans about how great it would be to sell but I wasn't doing anything to get there. It was as if I were 'sitting back and letting the money flow', which we know doesn't work.

As soon as I got home, I pulled out my notebook and made a list of people I knew who would know what to do. People who knew about this stuff. I remembered a friend who had mentioned someone he knew who ran an agency that made acquisitions, so I asked for an introduction. I knew of someone else who had sold his agency, so I messaged him for his availability. I set up conversations so I could find out how on earth I was going to do this.

I got these people on the phone and asked them hundreds of questions about what they had done. Antony, who had sold his agency, told me in detail about the process and how his team had made it a success. Tamara, with an agency about five times the size of mine, told me what she looked for when making acquisitions. That conversation was so valuable. Tamara was exactly the kind of buyer we were seeking, and she was generous with her time. I carried on doing this, and one conversation led to another. At some point in each chat came a 'Hey, you should speak to this person. I'll introduce you'. Before long I was introduced to the person who would introduce me to the person who would acquire us.

Planning your endgame means deciding exactly what you want and being intentional about making it happen. What's your ultimate goal? What's all this for? Define it and write it down. Then ask the question: 'How will I know?' If you don't define how you will know, the goalposts will keep moving. You might already be there, but you have not defined it well enough to realize your own success.

How will you know when to initiate your endgame? Perhaps it's when you have a certain daily routine. When you have finalized a specific deal. When you make a certain amount of money. When you have made a certain impact. Whatever it is, it has to be measurable. You have to know when it's happened. You have to know where you're trying to go.

Much of this is simply maths. How much do you need to have in assets to never have to work for money ever again?

Imagine your magic money number is $10 million. Selling a business for a 5-times multiplier means you'll need to be making $2 million per year in profit. But if you've been making healthy profits, much of your magic money number is already in the bank. You might not need a big exit.

Not only might you not need a big exit, but you might also not need that much in assets. Two million dollars in assets at a 5 per cent yield pays out $100,000 per year. How much does your dream life cost? (After you complete the next chapter's life designing exercise, you will know this.)

Think of your dream endgame and imagine hearing the news, realizing where you are, or seeing the goal happen. How does it feel? Picture how you will feel in that moment. Who will be with you, what will you be doing and wearing and what will your facial expression be? The next question is about you. What's the difference between the person you are now and the person who has achieved what you've written down? What's in the gap? Perhaps there's nothing in the gap and it's just a case of stepping into that version. Of acting like them and having their life.

If your ultimate goal is a sale, get sale-ready long before the event. Plan the endgame and spend the middle game building to sell. The policies and processes we covered earlier come into play here. Whenever you find yourself answering a question you've answered before, whenever you take something case by case, make a manual. Create solid business foundations upon which great people can flourish and great work can be delivered. Building scalable and saleable entities is what acquisition endgames require.

Setting up to sell

I have borrowed the following from the book *Exitpreneur*, by entrepreneur and business sale specialist Joe Valley. Valuable and saleable companies, he tells us, score highly across the following pillars:

- **Risk.** Scoring highly on the first pillar happens when your business is a solid purchase for a buyer and the risk is minimized. This pillar includes the size and age of your company; its defensibility against shocks; its dependencies, including on you as its owner; the channels through which it makes money and their associated risks; the risk of competition; and the risk of obsolescence.

- **Growth.** A buyer isn't buying your company's performance now but its potential. Demonstrating growth and growth potential means looking at top-line and bottom-line trends, and their future potential, timing and seasonality. A buyer will look for growth opportunities they can exploit, built-in paths to growth, and current or future investments that will pay off in the future.

- **Transferability.** If your business can only be run by you, it holds little value for someone else. Here's where a buyer looks at key personalities and key team members, to ensure there's a strong management structure in place. Also of note are relationships with manufacturers, the client or customer contracts, and the workload of every team member including the owners and any key partnerships, to ensure they transfer.

- **Documentation.** A buyer wants to buy a well-oiled machine, where the machine's instruction manual is clearly documented, not stored as tacit knowledge in your head. Here's where clear financials, logical accounting methods and robust contracts come in. Scoring well on this pillar happens when clear metrics are in place for the business as well as the existence and adherence to standard operating procedures (SOPs) detailing how every process should run.

- **The fifth pillar that isn't.** While not strictly a pillar, there's an element of magic involved in a business sale. Humans make buying decisions with their heart, then back up their decisions with their logical brain. The magic element involves you, as the owner of the business, being someone they want to do a deal with. Buyers have been known to overlook many elements of the first four pillars if they are hellbent on doing a deal. This can't be predicted or planned but it emphasizes how much everything is sales and everything you do contributes to your endgame in some way.

Tim Ferriss once said he wanted to 'own the trains but not be responsible for them running on time'. Operating like this from the start creates saleable businesses that are more valuable at the end and more fun to run in the middle. Managing a frantic, case-by-case operation that makes the same mistakes and repeatedly answers the same questions is no one's idea of a fulfilling career.

Rather than a sale, your endgame might be a business that you own but don't manage. Your endgame might be a business that's a dream to run, that you live an extraordinary life alongside.

A solid reputation, strong customer base and multiple positive reviews can contribute towards a lower-risk acquisition for a buyer. When policies and processes are in place, that helps with transferability. They also create a business that's more enjoyable to be part of, with fewer headaches and less time spent on admin.

Everything that makes your business more attractive to a buyer makes it more attractive to you as its owner.

Whatever it entails, your endgame should be on a need-to-know basis. When you tell someone, make sure there's a specific reason to. When the world knows your ulterior motive, whether it's an acquisition or lifestyle goal, you may find they undermine your work and what you're trying to do. Their knowledge may mean they raise objections or want to talk about your plans, rather than other, necessary conversations. Take daily steps in the right direction and disclose the right information to the right people at the right time. This will get you closer to your goal than sharing your plan with anyone who will listen.

Grandmasters of chess study the endgame. They set up boards of plausible combinations and practise those final few stages repeatedly. Whatever your endgame, it will not happen without a plan. Picture your dream scenario in your mind, decide how you'll know you're there, then step into the version of you that can make it happen.

Use an expert

For my agency's sale we partnered with a mergers and acquisitions broker. We had received an offer for purchase a few years before, but something hadn't felt right. The terms would have been good for me but not my team; the culture fit was all wrong. The potential buyer based the offer on targets that made no sense. They weren't clear about their intentions. I said no. It was about doing this right, not quickly.

In my business's case, the most important thing was the culture fit. Would our people get on with their people? Would it benefit our team and clients and be the best possible outcome for everyone? The agency's future success was important to me, as was the future of my team.

The mergers and acquisitions broker we chose to work with understood what we were looking for straightaway, and he had a few buyers in mind. In August 2020 we pressed go. In September we had 'chemistry meetings' with buyers from his extended network, which was vast. Many of those led to second meetings. Three put in offers. Our broker's team organized and negotiated on our behalf. They represented our best interests with every prospective deal. We got our perfect offer within five months of hiring the broker, and six weeks later we had completed the sale. Finding the right person in the right room can catapult plans into reality faster than you may have expected.

Finding a broker was the best decision I made. Speaking to someone for whom this process was routine filled me with confidence that a sale would happen. Some specialize in online businesses, some only work with agencies, but brokers exist in every industry. Finding people for whom your desired outcome of a sale is an everyday occurrence turns it from a pipe dream into a logical next step.

The future is now

Never stand still. Because why would you? Grow as a person, grow your network and remove bottlenecks to growth so that what you have built can scale beyond you. Dream bigger with your plans. Play at the top, where no one else has dared to go. Work out the difference between genuine opportunities and distractions in disguise. Make your personal policy of when to say yes and when to say no.

Picture your endgame and imagine it happening. Imagine someone buying your business for the exact amount you want. Imagine hearing the news that will change everything. Or imagine going ahead with that game-changing opportunity that will mark a huge milestone.

There is a version of you that exists in that reality. In the future. The difference between you and them is growth. All that's required is for you to grow into the person who can access it, and you might be closer to being that person than you think.

When I sold my agency, I was happy to stay but ready to go. I loved my team and clients. I wasn't desperate to leave. I thought about how content I was, doing what I was doing, and realized that the buyer would take on this feeling. My confidence meant I received better offers; potential buyers knew I wouldn't be low-balled. I never forgot what a great company they would be buying, which put me in a position of strength in negotiations. I happily would have walked away from the wrong deal.

The strongest negotiations are those where the seller is happy to walk away. The next chapter is how to make that happen.

Key takeaways

- Choose your area of mastery and make a plan for the others.
- Develop an accountability practice.
- Read with intention.
- Ask questions of the mentors in your mind.
- Grow your team proactively, rather than reactively.
- Don't rest on your laurels. Change your game when you are at the top of it.
- Don't complicate what is simple. Just start. The way will appear.
- Recognize when you are a bottleneck and remove yourself.
- Say yes when you should say yes, no when you should say no, and understand the difference.
- Think big. There's less competition.
- Pursue your endgame with action and expert help.

Supercharge your progress

Head over to the free *Ten Year Career* companion course for short videos and bonus downloads to apply this chapter's concepts and frameworks to your life and business.
Find it at jodiecook.com/TYC

9

Live By Design

• • •

The first time I checked my phone that morning I saw four missed calls from my general manager. Something had gone wrong. I called her back. 'Hey, are you okay?' I asked sleepily.

'Not really. The office was broken into last night, and all the computers are gone.'

I was in Toronto, Canada, five hours behind the UK. The break-in had happened 12 hours before, and my team had known for five. When they turned up to our office that morning, they found the door smashed and the computers, laptops and accessories gone. The thieves had left two old iMacs but taken the keyboards and trackpads that went with them. These criminals were fussy.

By the time we spoke, the team had sprung into action. They booked a door repair person. They called the police and reported the crime, notified our insurers and told the landlord. They remotely wiped all the stolen equipment. They went to Apple to replace the keyboards and trackpads so that two team members could work. The others had been called first thing and asked to work from home. A lot had happened while I was sleeping.

'Thanks for doing all that. Thanks for the update. Do you need me to do anything?'

'No. Later I'll make a plan for replacing all the computers and I'll run it by you, but everything is sorted for now.'

We hung up, and I sat there for a moment. Then I got on with my day. The fact that I was on the other side of the Atlantic didn't matter, even during a crisis. I saw that everything was as it should be, because the processes and people were in place to handle a moment just like this.

There are precursors of attitude and approach that are foundational to designing your life intelligently. In the first half of this chapter, I'll introduce each one. Then we'll get into the mechanics of the actual design:

- Playing a game
- Finding your tribe
- Showing up
- Letting go
- Euthymia
- Periodization and work–life balance
- Deciding what you're optimizing for.

Even if you don't see yourself as a lifestyle entrepreneur, enjoying life as a business owner and having a business that runs without daily struggles has clear benefits.

If your business is easier to run, not only is it more enjoyable to run but it's also easier to sell it to someone else. You will have less convincing to do. They will be ready to buy the asset you have created.

This is how to run a business without it running you.

Playing a game

How much you enjoy your life while running your business depends on many factors including your disposition, your support network and how intentional you are about living the life you want to lead.

Enjoyment matters, and it's achievable for all no matter how high the stakes. In mastering the art of running a business without it running you, a huge factor is how you view challenges. There's a stark difference between grumbling through the day judging every inconvenience, and gliding through, challenges and all. One feels like clambering uphill. One feels like fun.

If you measured success only by how much fun you were having, how would you score?

In my summer job at the print and promotion company, every time a new challenge occurred, my boss Simon was thrilled. He saw everything that came up as an exciting chance to learn. He would help me map out all available options. He taught me the best way to think about and deal with anything. No challenge that presented itself was bad.

Once you see running a business as playing a fun game, nothing can touch you. If you can say without doubt that you have put your all into every situation, nothing that happens can disturb your inner peace. Or your sleep. No comments from a team member, no email from a client, no troll on the internet. You sail through, you are generally very happy, and you always know what to do, or you know for sure that you'll figure it out.

Having fun is about being open, as opposed to closed. It's about having an open heart and an open disposition, about greeting every scenario with compassion and love and bringing your best self to every decision or negotiation. As soon as you have done everything you can, you let go because you choose to let go.

When our equipment was stolen while I was spending a month in Toronto, there would have been little point in me worrying about it while it was looked after by my team. If I focused on business being a challenging game and having gratitude for my team, no worry existed alongside.

When you are running a business it's easy to live in the future, where you tell yourself all will be okay after a certain point. 'I'll be happier when we've signed that deal', or 'I'll feel better when x happens.' There is no point in deferring enjoyment to a point in the future. What's more likely is that other things will crop up. When point x arrives, you forget you were supposed to be happy, and instead move the promise of happiness on to point y. This process repeats for ever until you look back and realize that you didn't enjoy your life all the time this was happening.

Once one challenge is over, another will appear. If there are no big challenges, smaller ones will appear bigger. You have no choice but to love the game. Tell yourself that you love it. One technique I like, no matter what happens, is to say 'Good' or 'Great' or another happy word. My work got deleted? Good, a chance to do it again better. We got broken into? Great. A chance to replace those iMacs with laptops. It's raining outside? Wonderful. The towpath will be less busy for my run.

When you meet both wonderful and adverse news with the same disposition, and back yourself to handle each, you will feel invincible.

Things will still fly at you, but where the pace used to feel relentless or overwhelming now you will take it all in your stride. You won't use unhelpful terms to describe the game you play.

You are better placed to deal with anything because not only have you trained your brain to see the positive side, you also see every challenge as a chance to grow. You approach every situation with an open disposition and bring your best self. You love what you do.

How you view challenges will also depend on the people you have around you.

Finding your tribe

Aimee felt uninspired.

She had started her coaching business and signed some clients but, ironically, was stuck herself. Her work was barrelling forward, but life wasn't following suit. She was going to the same places, seeing the same people and living each week on repeat. Her friends were getting married and having babies, and that wasn't her path. She craved new experiences and more excitement. She wanted life to sweep her off her feet. She wanted a change.

She would meet new men on dating apps, each of whom wasn't quite right. They weren't adventurous enough, she complained. They wanted to settle down and they bought their clothes from department stores. Their ambitions didn't go further than getting a promotion at work and getting wasted every weekend. This wasn't Aimee's idea of fun.

The trouble was, Aimee didn't know her idea of fun. She was looking to other people to define it for her. She realized that what she was seeking in a partner and friendship group was everything she was lacking in herself.

Aimee made the change. She wrote a list of all the things she was looking for in a dream partner and a dream group of friends. Then, instead of searching for those traits within other people, she created them within her own life. Instead of looking for someone who could make exciting plans, she made her own. Instead of looking for someone who was interesting and fun, she became more interesting and fun herself. Before, she would go along with what other people wanted to do.

Now, she defined her interests, became proud of who she was, and started doing only what she loved to do.

Aimee moved to Ibiza, her favourite place, and joined some Facebook groups, including one called Girl Gone International. Here she posted an introduction with her hobbies and asked if anyone wanted to meet for a coffee. She joined a coworking space and went along to the mixer events.

In doing this, Aimee started operating on a different frequency. She started attracting people just like the real her. In many chance encounters, she met people just like the ones she had described in her notebook.

Aimee found her tribe when she became her tribe.

Going against the grain – as you are doing in building your Ten Year Career – can be lonely. Remember I said you should expect to be seen as weird or odd? When everyone around you has different values, goals and versions of happiness or success, spending time with them is more a form of escapism than a source of inspiration or support. It's fine in small doses, but it won't keep you focused on what you need to do. For that, you need a tribe.

Finding a support network means finding people who are travelling a similar path and share similar values. Learning from each other, supporting each other, making introductions for each other. This support network isn't your clients or your social media followers. It's probably not the best friend you had at school. It may not be your family.

Most of the most successful people in the world have tight-knit friendships with a few people. They might know a lot of people, but their worries or challenges are reserved for the few, their core support team. The members of this team don't have to know each other.

My accountability group on Telegram, mentioned earlier, is a support network of like-minded people. The group has six members, and we work in similar ways. We share similar values. I know I could pick up the phone to anyone in the group and they would be there for me. We listen to each other, we coach each other, and it's made all the difference.

Finding your tribe, however small, changes how you feel every day and the person you become while running your business.

Birmingham, my hometown, has a network called Silicon Canal that runs a monthly tech drinks. When I went to those events, I felt that I'd found my tribe. Each attendee was casual and nerdy in the best possible way. We discussed ideas and challenges and laughed all evening. I would go home with my head buzzing and not be able to get to sleep. Someone without any interest in that group might have written off its members as boring, but no one is boring. Everyone has something interesting about them. Writing someone off as dull means you haven't found it yet.

Dynamite Circle is a similar vibe. It's a global network of location-independent entrepreneurs, many of whom were digital nomads before such a thing was cool. They had insane self-awareness and worked out how they could run a business and travel the world. Each member has a different story, and I love meeting them in random cities across the globe as well as in the forum.

There's no point sitting on the sofa wondering why your dream partner or friend isn't coming to find you. Instead, find yourself. Start doing the things that the best version of you does. The people who are also doing those things are your perfect tribe members.

Find your tribe, but first become your tribe. If you're looking for people to do fun things with, sign up to fun things first. If you want to find your type of person, start being your type of person. The more you start living life in a way that feels true to you, and the more you are honest about what you think and what you enjoy, the more you will attract people with shared interests. They will introduce you to other people they think you'd click with, and it goes from there. As Mahatma Gandhi said, 'We but mirror the world... As a man changes his own nature, so does the attitude of the world change towards him.' Be the change you want to see in the world and be your own best tribe member.

With the right foundations in place, you can show up in the right way.

Showing up

I want you to show up for everything. To be present wherever you have committed to be. Think of yourself as an artist honing your craft, not a dodgy dealer racing to the bottom to score a quick buck.

Showing up means learning to love everything you do, whether or not it comes naturally. Spiritual teacher and author Gabrielle Bernstein uses the concept of a 'super attractor'. When you focus on feeling good, when you show up for everything, you develop a superhuman aura. Like attracts like, so your incredible energy attracts incredible people and scenarios. Showing up means choosing to do something well even when you don't feel like it, because that's who you are.

It means jumping out of bed every morning no matter what's in your diary. It means greeting everyone with a smile no matter how you feel. It means approaching great news and adverse news in the same way. It means seeing the light in others that they can't see for themselves. Not looking for praise or recognition from any external source. Championing others while not needing the same in return.

How much you show up will dictate how much you can let go.

Letting go

Design your life around letting go.

One day during the last few years of owning my agency, I visited a friend. I was travelling back from her house when I had an urge to check in with my team. I was about to pick up my phone and call someone when I stopped myself. Was it necessary? My agency's managers knew what they were doing. They would let me know if they wanted my help. I trusted them. What would be the point in checking in right then?

Letting go when you want to delve in feels uncomfortable. Business owners rarely find it easy to train someone, then trust them to do a task while appreciating that they will add their own spin. But that's necessary. No leader wants to be a micromanager, but someone needs to earn their trust before being left to it. If the benchmark isn't in place, micromanaging could happen for ever. It leaves great team members frustrated, unable to develop autonomy and mastery, and brings only short-lived peace of mind for the owner.

How much you can let go is a direct result of how aware you are and the actions you have taken to delegate work. Learn where to let go, and then do it. Be unavailable often, while others have everything they need. Give them flexibility on decisions. It's impossible to pre-empt every problem but you can make the problem-solving framework solid. Hire based on character and attitude, and train the skills. Conscientious people don't need watching. They take pride in owning their role and excelling in their work.

If a leader can move past micromanaging, any tendencies to do it will likely be their gut telling them that something isn't right. The answer to that feeling is never to micromanage in response; it's either to train and trust, or to make a tough decision and find another person or supplier. Micromanaging is a blocker to growth and it means the wrong people are taking the place of the right people.

Euthymia

Comparison is the thief of joy.

Theodore Roosevelt Jr, US president

Especially with social media, it's so easy to feel as though the grass is always greener. In caveman times we would have gone about in small tribes. We wouldn't have known the daily achievements and news of everyone we had ever met.

Imagine you follow a thousand people across Instagram and Twitter, or whichever social networks you use. Imagine each of those 1,000 people shares something cool that happened to them once per year. Three times daily you'd see cool things other people were doing. Your brain wouldn't do the maths. Instead, you would believe subconsciously that amazing things happened to other people all the time. It would be easy to start comparing and feel inadequate or jealous.

Grass is greener syndrome might creep in and try to convince you there are other people who have it easier or are luckier. It might make you want to swap places. But it's false. Every career path has challenges; it's pointless seeing other journeys through rose-tinted glasses.

Envy is fear. It's fear that you don't have what someone else has, that you're missing out or not good enough. It's fear grounded in insecurity. When you wholeheartedly know your own path, fear slips away and doesn't reappear.

The opposite of envy is being genuinely happy for others without any form of resentment creeping in. Being inspired without idolizing. Critique without criticism. Avoiding comparison at all costs. Mike's app got a million downloads? Amazing! Sophie's book won an award? Wonderful news! I'm happy for them.

Whenever I'm in danger of falling into envy, I like to embrace the idea of 'euthymia', which is defined in Roman philosopher Seneca's essays as 'believing in yourself and trusting in your path, without following the myriad footpaths of those wandering in every direction'.

Even if someone else achieved that one thing that you'd give anything to have, at least now you know it's possible. Remember how I said I try to respond to every event with either 'good' or 'great'? This is what I mean; now you have an example of how it can be done. Good! Their journey could hold methods you haven't tried.

Find the good thing to say. When everyone else is putting someone down or judging their character, be the person who empathizes. When you feel a pang of envy at an acquaintance's milestone, possession or opportunity, practise sending happiness their way. Let their achievements be inspiration that, if it's possible for them, it's possible for you. Remind yourself that they are travelling their path as you are travelling yours. Euthymia.

Being crystal clear on your purpose will mean you never need to sway from your path. Find the answers to the big questions: what am I here to do? What do I stand for? How do I want to spend my time? Live the answers to those questions and become the kind of person who inspires others and makes them want to up their game.

Periodization and work–life balance

In powerlifting, athletes' training plans follow the concept of periodization: a five-or-so-week training block, including a de-load week of recovery. During the training weeks the volume and/or intensity of lifts builds up. During de-load weeks volume is reduced. Periodization occurs throughout our lives: in the seasons, in economic cycles, in financial markets, in the sowing and reaping of crops.

You are you. If you bring your best self to every table, you are the same body and mind in every situation. You don't suddenly become a different person when the clock hits 5 pm, or when you land in a new sunny place. Living your most authentic self in every situation is freeing; the alternative feels false. It marks a lack of integrity.

The concept of work–life balance to me means committing to work or to rest, and not hanging out in a confused middle. When I work, I work. I listen to concentration music, block out distractions and turn off notifications. It gets intense. I'm at 100 per cent of my focus and determination capacity, so the words are written and the processes finished.

When I train, I train. The phone goes away, I turn the music up, and I focus on lifting weights, completing a session, and bringing my mind back if it starts to wander. It's tempting to check your emails when taking a day of rest. Or in the middle of the night. It's easy to scroll Instagram while stretching, have WhatsApp open while working, or be daydreaming while playing with the kids. How often have you been on a Zoom call where someone is typing while you are talking, or vice versa? Multitasking or letting life drift into work and back again means doing many things to a mediocre standard. That's not the stuff excellence is made of.

Life can have ten-year phases that are clearly defined, but every 90 days your life might look different from the previous 90 days. That's periodization in action. On a micro-level, your day can include periodization. Following your natural energy levels means you work and relax at your optimal time. Each day is designed and every action feels effortless because you know how to match your actions with your disposition. Include both intense work and committed rest.

See your day as chunks of time in which to immerse yourself in whatever you are doing. Creative work, managerial work, exercise, cooking, reading, meditating, playing with your kids, learning something new. Batch activities such as administrative tasks, responding to tweets or planning your next actions, rather than letting those expand across a day. Low-quality days consist of low-level focus across multiple areas instead of the more optimal batched focus and single-track activities.

Work–life balance means protecting the boundaries between what you do because multitasking is ineffective. See your year in chunks of time, where you know what you will achieve in each quarter. See your life in ten-year-long chunks, where you define each decade and its focus.

Deciding what you're optimizing for

To enter this competition simply complete this form with your email address, full name and phone number, follow us on Twitter, like our Facebook page, subscribe to our YouTube channel and post us three drops of a unicorn's blood. Don't forget to include a stamped addressed envelope.

As part of the work carried out for our clients, my agency regularly designed and ran contests across their social media pages. Contest entries could require an email address, a like on a page or post, or answering a question. One submission counted as one entry to the competition, and they were often very popular.

We knew, however, that for every additional step an entrant was required to complete, the drop-off rate – the people who simply clicked away and didn't finish their submission – increased. We faced a trade-off. Do we just require an email address from entrants and gather many more potential leads? Do we ask for more information and reduce those leads to more committed fans? Do we use the competition as an opportunity to grow our fans and followers, or grow our contact base? 'Chase two rabbits,' as the old proverb says, 'catch neither.'

Our clients didn't always like having to prioritize and reduce the entry requirements, but it was necessary. To get the results we were after, we resolved to narrow our focus.

There are trade-offs in every decision. Going down one path means forgoing another.

You might have already experienced trade-offs. In weight training there's often a trade-off between training for strength and training for aesthetics. Another in training for size or training for agility. For a bigger one-rep max or for increased endurance.

Consider the role of prime minister. The role earns an above-average salary and provides the opportunity to make a huge difference in the world, at the expense of their privacy. The prime minister might affect the world but not see their family as much as they'd like. Plus, they're at the mercy of the media and open to scrutiny in everything they do. Trade-offs.

One of my friends is living her version of an extraordinary life by teaching English in Spain. She has long afternoons off, doesn't work weekends, is in year-round sunshine and has great friends around her. But she doesn't earn very much. She's aware that earning more might come at the cost of the lifestyle she's grown to love, so she's cool with that.

Along the journey of your Ten Year Career, you will face daily trade-off decisions. Going one way over another, spending your day in meetings or working solo, choosing which favour to ask that one person, pursuing a new avenue versus putting energy into the existing one – these are a few of the questions that will be asked of you. Only you can decide the best route forwards.

There always will be invitations and things you could do. Others will want you to start side projects with them, customers will want a custom version of your offering, and you will be asked to speak at events and sit on panels. If you optimize for spreading yourself thinly, you should do all these things. If you optimize for your Ten Year Career, consider what you will, by default, leave behind with each step forward. Leaving behind old commitments, obligations and people that don't fit your life now is fine. Leaving behind your hopes and dreams while you fulfil obligations is not.

Will you skip your morning run if a team member needs you? Will you forgo a flash car to reinvest profits into advertising? Will you check your emails during a meal with your best friend? Will you cover shifts and postpone your business expansion plans? Which trade-offs are you prepared to make, and which are hard limits?

Designing your life means that, as well as defining its contents, you define what doesn't matter to you. You don't try to optimize for everything.

Intentional designing

'Would you tell me, please, which way I ought to go from here?'
'That depends a good deal on where you want to get to,' said the Cat.
'I don't much care—' said Alice.
'Then it doesn't matter which way you go,' said the Cat.
'—so long as I get somewhere,' Alice added as an explanation.
'Oh, you're sure to do that,' said the Cat, 'if you only walk long enough.'

Lewis Carroll, *Alice's Adventures in Wonderland*

If you intentionally see yourself as playing a game rather than working hard, you keep perspective, even when the game feels tough. You will see challenges as fun puzzles rather than reasons to despair. You will be a joy to be around, and you might start to enjoy your own company more. Finding the nearest distraction – a phone, a news site or a television show – won't be a priority because you can hang out with your own thoughts, which no longer cause you worry.

Finding your tribe happens when you intentionally think and act like your dream tribe member. Instead of waiting for someone to fill gaps, you fill them yourself and meet people doing the same. Showing up means being there, present and ready for anything. Alert, switched on and missing nothing. 'You see, but you do not observe,' said fictional detective Sherlock Holmes. I want you to observe every detail of your Ten Year Career and the extraordinary life it creates.

Letting go of the need to control what is being taken care of, letting go of the need to be liked or feared, and letting go of past versions of yourself all propel you forward. You're not losing yourself, you're finding yourself. Like a phoenix rising from the ashes, if you like. You have intentional breakthroughs, not accidental breakdowns. The concept of euthymia brings the courage to disregard any path other than your own. Your career is neither a race nor a dress rehearsal. Every day is your unique chance to be unapologetically you.

Working until you crash is not the path. Seek a sustainable everyday you could keep up for ever. Incorporating periodization puts this into context. Work and life move in seasons; there are winters and summers as there are sprints and rests. Intentionally defining those seasons in advance means you can act accordingly when each arrives.

Prioritization is your friend. Just as you cannot be all things to all people, trying to do too much too well is a false economy. Do less but do it better. Work out what is important to you and forget the rest. Choose the metrics that match your goals to get a true sense of your standing on the important stuff.

Every part of your Ten Year Career, and the phases thereafter, should be something you design intentionally. Although this sounds simple, it's not that common. How many business owners are guilty of making goals for their business but not their life? Meticulously booking calls or meetings but leaving their holiday plans to the last minute. Investing in machinery but not in friendships. They see life as something that happens when they're not working. Weekends are there to kill time between workdays.

You might have heard the phrase 'life is what happens when you're making other plans'. Without a clear picture of what your ideal life looks like, no amount of designing or planning will get you there, because you don't know where there is. If you leave it to chance, you'll be distracted with arbitrary events, other people's plans for your time and whatever is going on in the news.

Get intentional about defining your extraordinary life. Operate within the caveat that it has to be your version, not what someone else thinks you should do and not what will make you look good on Instagram. Consider no one else's opinion. This life is for your benefit and not for anyone watching.

The opposite of living by design is living by default. It's where life happens to you and you go with the flow. A life lived by default feels frustrating, like being pulled along or controlled like a puppet. Seek design, not default.

In your most extraordinary life, filled with only those things you love to do, picture how you feel. Picture what you're doing, who you're with, what you're wearing, what life smells like. Picture opening your calendar and seeing what your week involves.

In the rest of this chapter, I'll introduce you to specific techniques for designing your life:

- Booking it to make it happen
- Planning your daily routine
- Completing a lifestyle design exercise
- Deciding your not-to-do list
- Accessing a first-class experience.

Booking it

Whatever you think you can do or believe you can do, begin it – for action has magic, grace and power in it.
            Johann Wolfgang von Goethe, poet and dramatist

The clock had struck midnight on 31 December 2014 in Australia and Sydney Harbour Bridge was celebrating in style. Six tonnes of fireworks were exploding in perfect harmony across the bridge, the harbour and the opera house. This countdown marked the start of my first month away, a time when I would live and work from another country. Watching the sky light up and the music blare, I thought about how close I had been to not booking this trip. It was in my calendar, but it was negotiable. I told my team I wouldn't go if they needed me. I didn't book the flights until the last minute.

I was scared of what might happen when I was gone. I was scared of the 10-hour time difference that would mean my team could only reach me at certain times. While I was deliberating about making the booking, a friend challenged me: 'What's the worst that could happen?'

I wrote a list of all the bad things that could happen. Then I wrote a list of what I would do in each scenario. It really wasn't that bad, so I booked the trip.

I was wrestling between the part of me that wanted to run a great business and the part of me that wanted to travel the world. I hadn't realized that not only could I have both, each would complement the other. Unless life plans are set in stone, they won't happen. Other things will crop up.

For a business owner there's never a good time to go away, and there's always at least one reason to stay. But once you make the plans, everything falls into place and you set off with a sense of peace. From January 2015 to March 2020 my husband and I spent one month of every three living and working from a different city. We worked away for four months of every year, without fail. Our destinations included Cape Town, Bali, Sydney, Austin, Vancouver, Berlin and Stockholm. I never once regretted a trip.

One business owner I know spends one weekend every month staying at a local hotel with his family. It's the same weekend each time but a different hotel. They relax in the spa, explore the grounds and have dinner and breakfast in each other's company. Phones go away. It's a family tradition that does not move under work pressures.

Author Dan Meredith has a weekly calendar booking that he calls a 'dentist appointment'. There is no real appointment: it's the space he takes for reflection. It's where he takes a step back to think about what he's doing and why. It's for self-awareness and pausing. He looks forward to these slots, and his assistant knows they are immovable.

Parkinson's law says that work expands to fill the time available. If life isn't planned, work will fill any gaps. It's inevitable. The best way to be more productive is to narrow your working time, not expand it.

Chances are you'll get more done. Regular trips, treats and rests will lead to maximizing your work time and achieving more, not less.

What's standing between you and your dream life? Perhaps just a few bookings.

Daily routine

Routines are easier to maintain than create. Remember how many daily thoughts humans have that are exactly the same as the day before? Those thoughts lead to the same words and actions. Changing actions and habits requires interventions.

Habits remove the need for willpower. A daily routine is a series of habits that ensure your life and work schedules are designed. Small changes can make a big difference to your happiness and productivity.

Maybe you hate commuting. Question why you work where you do and what other options you have. Can you move closer to where you work or arrive and leave earlier to avoid the traffic instead? Maybe you hate grocery shopping. Can you automate a weekly shop? Looking at your life objectively to make changes is the crux of lifestyle design. That's how you live by design and not by default. I'm amazed at how few people actually think about these things or consciously make these decisions. Living by default is, well, the default.

I've talked about the concept of a victory hour, which refers to the first hour upon waking, and how you spend it having huge bearing on the rest of your day. But what about your last hour before bed? Scrolling your phone until lights out isn't conducive to restful sleep. Most phones have wind-down modes; perhaps you could set a reminder when it's time to do certain things. Maybe your wind-down routine involves comfy clothes, a good book, a certain type of music or a candle. Perhaps it means sitting on the sofa resting. Whatever the routine, commit it to paper and question how well it's setting up your sleep.

Designing exercise

Most bucket lists have no indication of when things will happen, but someday isn't a real day. Take a piece of paper and create columns with the headings: every day, every other day, every week, every month, every quarter, every year. Then underneath each of these headings, write down the things you want to do at these frequencies.

Don't just include the big things. Your list doesn't have to be only elaborate trips or lavish entertainment. Include the little things that you might take for granted, like taking walks, seeing your friends, napping, being in nature, and whatever else fills you with joy. What are those things you love to do that always wait until you have a spare moment, a moment that never seems to arrive?

Your list should only contain stuff that your actual self wants to do. Two things that should not be on it are (a) what someone else thinks you should do or (b) what I'll call 'legacy goals'. Maybe your parents wanted you to be a doctor, or your friend wants you to go with them to see that band they love but you don't. Leave it off the list. Whenever you hear the word 'should', notice. It's social programming, guilty or needless obligation at play.

Legacy goals are things you 'always wanted to do' and relate to the wants and needs of your former self, not your current self. Maybe your younger self dreamt of living in Australia or completing an Ironman; you think you still want those things but you actually don't. Recognize them as legacy goals and leave them off the list.

When you're writing your list, think about sustainability and consistency. The goal is that every day contains things that you want to do and that you could replicate this day over and over. This piece of paper, once filled in, represents you doing exactly what you want to do with the time you have on this planet.

Once you have this, cost it all out. Assign a cost to every item and then add it up for the year. When I worked this out for myself, it was a huge moment. I realized it was inexpensive. Accessible. You don't need to be a millionaire to live a millionaire's life, or your version of a millionaire's life.

Not-to-do list

Imagine you sit down to do three important things in the next few hours. You open your email and see ten emails from other people with the things that they want you to do for them. How many times have you forgone your plans to address such requests, only to realize you haven't touched your own list? That's definitely happened to me.

If we're not careful, our lives can look like a scaled-up version of a full inbox, an existence in which we defer our priorities in favour of flitting about answering to other people. Even once you've made your extraordinary life plan and you have a good idea what you want your days to contain, that plan is not the default until you make it so.

My dad's advice, whenever I was feeling busy running an agency, was to always do the thing that made the most difference to my business first. Do it, then do the next thing that makes the most difference. Running a to-do list that way gives a clear sense of priority. It means if anything is left, it's inconsequential.

If I want to live an extraordinary life, I need to be intentional about it every single day; otherwise it won't happen. Your only finite resource is time. There is always a way of earning more money. Everyone running a business or working for one that's growing can always add more value to be worth more.

A more important list to write is a not-to-do list. This includes all those things that you don't want to do. My not-to-do list includes household chores and cooking. Plenty of people love cooking, but it's not my thing. Plenty of people love vacuuming, but it's not my thing. This is about defining what is on your not-to-do list and removing it from your day-to-day. For everything on the list you have three options: delegate, automate, eliminate. In the words of Tim Ferriss, 'Never automate something that can be eliminated, and never delegate something that can be automated.'

I want clean floors; I can't drop that. I could delegate by hiring a cleaner to vacuum. Instead, I automate. In my house is a robot vacuum cleaner. This robot works on my schedule, vacuum-cleaning my house while I'm out. The cute little thing does what I won't. Cost: £300. Time saved: 15 minutes, every few days, for the rest of my life.

Once you start thinking this way, you can get creative with removing things you don't want to do from your life. It's liberating. It clears space for what matters.

The first-class experience

You don't need to join the masses, even for simple everyday things. It's always possible to buy a first-class experience. Upgrade your ticket. Join a more expensive club with fewer members. Only eat at Michelin-starred restaurants. Hire someone else to run your errands.

Another way is by simply switching your timings. The supermarket is busiest at the weekends. The gym is busiest on weekday evenings. The restaurant is packed at 7:30 pm but dead between 5 and 7 pm.

Work early in the morning. Go to the gym in the afternoon. Book the early slot for dinner. Go for a run on Saturday evening. When you do what everyone is doing, you have to share the space, the chefs, the roads, the changing rooms.

For a business owner there is rarely a good reason to do something when everyone else is. There's no need to succumb to the default and often unquestioned schedule of the week. If you want to meditate at 11 am, do it. If that idea fills you with dread, work out why. What's broken? If you were in a meeting for an hour and uncontactable by anyone, you wouldn't have the same dread. So why does taking rest time within a weekday feel different? Guilt? Obligation? Dig into that feeling and work out what needs to change.

When you have true control over how you spend your time, you can have first-class experiences every day. It leads to a first-class life. Upgrade your reality while living within your means.

Design your life

Doing work that doesn't feel like work is how you win at life. Feeling retired without being retired is part of the game.

You deserve to live a sustainable everyday that you don't need to escape. My goal, and the goal of this book, is that the best version of you arrives every morning and looks forward to the day ahead.

When our work feels like a choice we make every day, it takes a different form. It's no longer the time of our week we dread. We happily talk about work over dinner because no conversation topic can disturb our peace. When each encounter, email, problem or deal is a reason to smile, no matter the content, something changes. I'm not saying ignore problems or pretend that late delivery driver hasn't irked you, but I am saying you are a reflection of the world you choose to see. Take ownership of everything in your life, including your work, and resolve either to make a change or enjoy its presence. The middle ground – long, unfulfilling labour that you don't really enjoy – is no fun at all.

We can create the life we want to lead, starting today.

Run your business without it running you. Enjoy every day and be a delight to be around because you are so assured in yourself. Find your tribe to never feel alone. Know when to show up and when to let go. Avoid envy of anyone else's path by knowing your own passion and purpose. Take only inspiration from others; give only encouragement.

Get intentional about designing your life in the same way that you plan your business goals and processes. Map it, cost it, book it. There is no other way. Working within constraints forces prioritization. It forces the creation of a routine that serves you and elimination of the nonessential.

Making your vocation your vacation is what creates an extraordinary life. You'll recognize it when your working cadence is sustainable and when you feel as though you're playing a challenging game instead of battling uphill. You'll recognize it when something is going on thousands of miles away in your business and you know that it will be fine.

Working towards your ideal lifestyle over working towards retirement makes the journey sustainable and loveable. Not only that, but your ideal lifestyle is achievable right now. Ironically, by becoming intentional about your lifestyle and setting up your career in this way, you might be so happy that you feel as if you already have retired.

Key takeaways

The prerequisites to designing the life you want are:
- Playing a fun game.
- Finding your tribe.
- Showing up.
- Letting go.
- Euthymia.
- Periodization.

With those in place, take the steps to design your life:
- Plan your dream day and year.
- Cost it out and book it in.
- Define your not-to-do list.
- Create your own first-class experience.

Design your life then live it

Head over to the free *Ten Year Career* companion course for short videos and bonus downloads to apply this chapter's concepts and frameworks to your life and business.
Find it at jodiecook.com/TYC

10

The Ten Year Career Framework

● ● ●

Wherever you are right now, within ten years you could not need to work.

This is the framework by which you can complete a Ten Year Career or fast-track to freedom on your terms.

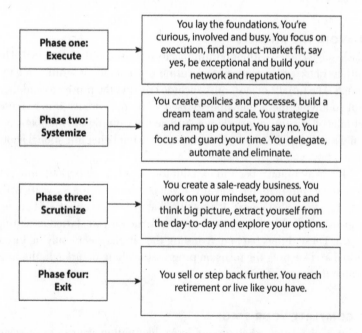

During my Ten Year Career I spent the first three years in phase one, years four to six in phase two, six to nine in phase three and six months in phase four. We will each travel a different path. There is no one-size-fits-all for this method and definitely no right or wrong.

Maybe you'll spend longer in one phase and less time in another. Maybe you'll hit upon something huge really quickly and complete the whole game much faster. Maybe you'll love living in phase three and continue there indefinitely.

What now?

1 WORK OUT WHERE YOU ARE

Where are you in your Ten Year Career journey? Execute, systemize, scrutinize or exit? Think of your business, your responsibilities and your day-to-day, then read the descriptions of each stage and get clear on where you sit. Perhaps you're in the trenches of one, transitioning between two or straddling multiple stages. Self-awareness is all that matters here.

2 AVOID THE PITFALLS

Each stage comes with opportunities to seize and pitfalls to avoid. The pitfalls of execute include not executing well enough or scrutinizing too much. The pitfalls of systemize include creating the processes and then not following them, allowing yourself to be pulled back into execute. Pitfalls of scrutinize include not sufficiently running the numbers, not fully knowing what you want and therefore not being intentional about if and how you move to exit.

It's okay to have been in execute for an extended period; now you can make your plan. It's okay if you've been scrutinizing for years without deciding what's next. It's totally okay if you executed, systemized and scrutinized and then a market shock meant you started executing again. These things happen. Avoiding the pitfalls means staying intentional and keeping the focus on progressing along in order, in the time frame that works for you.

3 COMPLETE YOUR STAGE

Paint a picture of what success looks like within your current stage, then work on that and that alone. Within execute, it could be a specific revenue milestone or a certain number of inbound enquiries every week. Perhaps it's a certain number of documented processes that are followed perfectly if systemize is your place. For scrutinize, success might mean having full clarity on your way forward, or having successfully exited your business if you're in the fourth and final stage of the framework.

4 PROGRESS TO THE NEXT
When you have completed your stage, make your plan for progressing to the next. Execute to systemize means hiring, training and automating to remove yourself as a blocker to growth. Systemize to scrutinize means getting perspective on your well-oiled machine to decide your next move. Scrutinize to exit means taking the leap with selling or completely removing yourself from the running of your business.

Your onward journey

In *Ten Year Career* companion course we deep dive into the framework and what it means for you. We'll assess which stage you are in and where to go from there. The companion course includes a detailed plan for each stage, the beliefs to hold in each one, as well as how to ensure you avoid the pitfalls.
Find the companion course at jodiecook.com/TYC

Conclusion: Over To You

In a parallel universe, your old self hits snooze on their alarm clock.

Feeling groggy, you reach for your phone and check the news, the weather and your social media accounts. You groan as you think about the day ahead and what it entails, reminding yourself that it's nearly the weekend. Thank goodness. You get up and peer in the mirror at the out-of-shape, fatigued and uninspiring sight before you, promising to book a holiday, get some exercise and start that project you've been thinking about for years.

You get in your battered car and drive to an uninspiring yet over-priced office, hitting rush-hour traffic on the way and turning on the radio to distract your mind. Luckily, the news reports something of note, and escapism ensues. The workday includes meetings that could have been phone calls and phone calls that could have been emails. You fly off the handle at a supplier and feel irritable all morning. Your employees ask questions they have asked before and you spend the afternoon putting out fires that shouldn't have started.

Run a business, they said. It'll be fun.

A few new orders come in, a few customer interactions take place, and a bit of creativity is required during a meeting. Someone brought cakes in for their birthday. Nothing truly ground-breaking happens. Mainly you monotonously punch the keyboard and make small talk until it's time to go home.

This repeats, every day, for decades. Your shadow self reaches state-pension age and wonders where the time went. You think of all those chances you could have taken, all those times you played it safe, and all the times you were busy being busy instead of intentionally being focused.

This isn't you. This wasn't me.

By working through the phases outlined in this book, including planning my endgame, the acquisition of my social media agency happened exactly as I envisioned. The agency I had started in a spare room with a laptop and a dream was acquired with a team of wonderful people, hundreds of happy clients (including local businesses and household name brands), 200-plus five-star Google reviews, and more opportunities for everyone involved.

My mindful progress through the scrutinize phase of my Ten Year Career led to the realization that I wanted to remove myself as owner and remove a ceiling, for myself and my team. Today, the company I founded is no longer confined by my vision of how big I want it to grow or what kind of work I think we should do. The team is capable and ambitious. We have outgrown each other.

My Ten Year Career won't look like yours because we each travel our own paths. Yours is for you to create.

Maybe you won't sell your business and sail off into the sunset. Maybe you'll have the realization that you are already living your dream life. Maybe you'll go for bigger opportunities or become more intentional about each day. I hope your next year is unrecognizable from the last, in the best possible way.

I don't know for sure what will happen next in your life and career, but I know it's going to be great. Stay open to opportunity and remember you always have the freedom to choose. The freedom to be whatever you want and spend each day however you wish. The funny thing is, like Dorothy in *The Wizard of Oz*, you had that power all along.

Most people, even business owners, ride a conveyor belt that they don't question. They strive to be on the side of the majority, seek the safety of familiarity and comfort, and avoid standing out, lest people stare. But standing out is inevitable for those making their mark, and questioning is the most valuable tool in your toolbox. With the right questions, you can find all the answers you're looking for. A Ten Year Career, making your mark in a big way in a shorter space of time, fast-tracking to freedom – it's all possible. I believe in you.

You are here, on this tiny planet in a huge galaxy, once and once only. Experiment, play and see what's possible. Be one of the rare few who truly find out what you are capable of.

'Normal' does not exist. Limits do not exist. Traditions and customs and 'should' and 'ought to' don't mean anything. You do you, whether they like it or not. It's your life and these are your choices. It's your path, your Ten Year Career. There you are, in the arena. Not on the sidelines, not a critic of those in the arena, not gossiping or speculating or tentatively dipping a toe in, but fully in, completely immersed, giving your all to living an extraordinary life.

What are you capable of? Think back to a big goal you achieved. Do you remember the process that led up to it? You set the goal and you made it happen. You planned how to get there, you put the hours in, and you didn't give up.

Get in your imaginary helicopter, fly it up to 10,000 feet and look at your life from afar. Close your eyes and talk to your imaginary mentors about what you could do. Write a journal entry from your future self, about the life you live, and work back from there.

Fast-tracking to freedom requires working out a plan, directing your energy, and being intentional about what you want to do. I'm no superhero; this is replicable. The journey you have now completed in reading this book has walked you through key elements of making it happen.

First, we visited the lies we live, the education conveyor belt and the decisions we make without question. I addressed the times we stay in line and explained why they will not set you up for success.

Next, we looked into the alternative way to be. There are regular people living extraordinary lives because they decided enough was enough and they made what they wanted to happen, happen. Finding examples is proof that it's possible for you. These people are happy to share, and in Chapter 2 we learned from their stories.

We reimagined reality. What are you capable of? Much more than you give yourself credit for. Most people operate within their comfort zone and panic when the perimeter stretches. The answer lies in pushing your edges and looking for opportunities to do so. If you want what no one else has, do what no one else will do.

Your trusted accompaniment on this journey is your mind, and it can help or hinder you depending on how it's programmed. Chapter 4, 'Your mind matters', introduced the lizard brain and the voice in your head that has no place in your career. Intuition and gut, sure, but self-sabotage and compulsion will not serve your best life.

Next, we set up for success, laying the foundation from which excellence can happen. Positioning, planning, consistency of actions and chalking up one solid performance after another. We looked at the four phases of the Ten Year Career framework to work out where to focus and when. We touched on being exceptional in everything you do.

We talked about sales, and how sales are everything. Creating a company or becoming a person that people want to buy from consists of playing the giving game, following up and tracking, while not being afraid to be a little naive. Consistency continues throughout sales because it builds your brand as reputable and trusted.

We looked at why hope is not a strategy and why there are no silver bullets. Practice makes permanent, and every action must match the person you want to be. There is only one you, so craft who you are. We covered focus, ideas and developing policies for every aspect of your work. Success is not an accident.

Chapter 8 dug into growth, which means never standing still, being ready to adapt. Have growth in mind, because what's the alternative? You learned how growing as a person, through mastery, accountability and learning, is part of a Ten Year Career. That includes growing your network and growing your team, removing blockers to growth and removing yourself as a bottleneck in any area. Planning your endgame and aligning your actions, while remembering that it's simple.

The idea of designing your life threads through the entire book, but is the particular focus in Chapter 9. Set up your days, weeks, months and years so that you are the person you want to be, living the life you want to live. Live by design or live by default. Here we got geeky with life planning, deciding what you're optimizing for, organizing it and booking it. Create a not-to-do list and run your business without it running you. Above all, trust in your path and don't follow those wandering in every direction.

Finally, the Ten Year Career framework will help you work out where you are and what your next move should be.

We covered a lot. The tools are in your hands; what you do with them is up to you. You have the power to make your mark in ways you might not yet be able to imagine. The power is within you right now, waiting for you to tap into it. You won't find it in envy, complaining or judgement. You won't find it copying others, gossiping, scrolling social media or watching television. You will find it when you move past the ordinary, mundane tasks that are trying to steal your days.

So what should you do? Start by journalling and visualizing. What would it feel like to live the life of your dreams? What would it look like, smell like, taste like? On the journey of your Ten Year Career, what would your days hold? What signs would show you that you were heading in the right direction? How would you know you had arrived, and what would that mean for you and everyone around you?

Then write down the exact questions you are looking for the answers to. Trust those answers will find you.

Let this be the reminder you need that anything is possible. There are no boundaries, there are no limits, there is no spoon. If you can visualize it happening and put the action in to match, you can work it into existence.

Revisit the lessons in the book as often as you need to. Any time you feel yourself being swayed or sucked into something you *should* do, or *always have* done, revisit the messages. Remember there is another way. I will be here rooting for you on every step of your journey, your personal mentor, much-needed reminder and eternal hype girl. The freedom you seek is waiting to be discovered.

If you haven't already, visit jodiecook.com/TYC to access the free *Ten Year Career* companion course. Here you will find video walkthroughs, worksheet downloads and how-to guides plus many more resources to fast-track your progress and make your Ten Year Career happen. I look forward to seeing you there.

Let's do this.

Bibliography

Beveridge, Harriet and Hunt-Davis, Ben, *Will It Make The Boat Go Faster?: Olympic-winning Strategies for Everyday Success*, 2nd edn (Matador, 2020)

Carnegie, Dale, *How to Win Friends and Influence People*, special edn (Vermilion, 2012)

Clear, James, *Atomic Habits: An Easy and Proven Way to Build Good Habits and Break Bad Ones* (Random House, 2018)

Cook, Jodie, *Instagram Rules: The Essential Guide to Building Brands, Business and Community* (Frances Lincoln, 2020)

Cook, Jodie, *Stop Acting Like You're Going to Live Forever: Guided Journal* (independently published, 2020)

Cook, Jodie and Daniel Priestley, *How to Raise Entrepreneurial Kids* (Rethink Press, 2020)

Coyle, Daniel, *The Culture Code: The Secrets of Highly Successful Groups* (Random House Business, 2019)

Ferriss, Timothy, *The 4-Hour Workweek: Escape the 9–5, Live Anywhere and Join the New Rich* (Vermilion, 2008)

Fields Millburn, Joshua and Nicodemus, Ryan, *Minimalism: Live a Meaningful Life* (Asymmetrical Press, 2011)

Greene, Robert, *The 48 Laws of Power* (Profile Books, 2000)

Horowitz, Ben, *The Hard Thing about Hard Things: Building a Business When There Are No Easy Answers* (Harper Business, 2014)

Itzler, Jesse, *Living with a Seal: 31 Days Training with the Toughest Man on the Planet* (Center Street, 2015)

Keller, Gary, *The One Thing: The Surprisingly Simple Truth behind Extraordinary Results: Achieve Your Goals with One of the World's Bestselling Success Books* (John Murray Learning, 2014)

Kishimi, Ichiro and Fumitake Koga, *The Courage to Be Disliked: How to Free Yourself, Change Your Life and Achieve Real Happiness* (Allen & Unwin, 2018)

Kiyosaki, Robert, *Rich Dad, Poor Dad: What the Rich Teach Their Kids about Money That the Poor and Middle Class Do Not!*, 2nd edn (Plata, 2017)

McKeown, Greg, *Essentialism: The Disciplined Pursuit of Less* (Virgin Books, 2021)

Schwartz, David J., *The Magic of Thinking Big* (Vermilion, 2008)

Sharma, Robin, *The 5AM Club* (HarperCollins, 2018)

Sivers, Derek, https://sive.rs/nowff (Now page)

Stone, Brad, *The Everything Store* (Corgi, 2014)

Valley, Joe, *The EXITPreneur's Playbook: How to Sell Your Online Business for Top Dollar by Reverse Engineering Your Pathway to Success* (Lioncrest Publishing, 2021)

Wallman, James, *Stuffocation: Living More with Less*, 1st edn (Penguin Life, 2017)

Acknowledgements

Everything in this book was made possible by the wonderful JC Social Media crew. Every team member, client, supplier or referrer, thank you for the part you played in the last ten years. A lot of people championed and supported us throughout every stage of our journey.

There are so many people to thank, and I am grateful for every single one of you. David and Joanna especially, thanks for trusting me and for being exceptional people I am proud to have worked with for so long. Thanks to Darren and James for taking what we built and dreaming even bigger. I'm excited for the future of every team member under your leadership. David B, thanks for the introductions and expert guidance, and for making it look easy. John Moore, a trusted friend who happens to be an accountant, thank you for always understanding. I was lucky to have won the parent lottery and was raised in a home designed so the default was possibility, confidence and speaking our minds. Growing up, my sister and I knew no limits and we had no fears; there were only ever reasons to be happy. These are the habits that underpin everything, and I will never underestimate their effect. Mum, Dad and Lucy, thanks for making it so.

In writing and editing this book I took many long walks with friends during which we paced the canals of Birmingham and I tested the ideas and stories enclosed within. Lydia, Nic, Yagmur, Jez, Jess and Anisa, thank you for your help, feedback and patience.

Thanks to each member of my kick-ass accountability group. Graham, Sophie, Dave, Christina and Mark – you are the best. Having you as sounding boards, for advice and encouragement, has made all the difference through this year and you all inspire me. What are we capable of?!

Thank you Derek Sivers for the constant inspiration and the generous foreword. Thanks for reminding me that it really can be simple.

Thank you to my editor, Hal Clifford, for upping my writing game and giving the most direct of feedback. Hal, you listened, understood and expertly transformed the manuscript, giving structure to the mess of concepts in my head.

Many thanks to the team at John Murray Learning, particularly Jonathan Shipley, Jen Campbell, Purvi Gadia and Diana Talyanina. Thank you Sarah Christie for the wonderful book cover.

Thank you to everyone who opened a door, made an introduction or put in a good word. There are so many of you. Paul Bayliss, Rob Bhol, Paul Burgess, Alex Bishop, Joel Blake, Nick Bonnaud, Suzie Branch-Haddow, Duncan Cheatle, David Clarke, Nigel Clegg, Sue Froggatt, Tim Edwards, Steve Hollis, Rob Geraghty, Antony Green, Carrie Green, Judith Greenburgh, Simon Greenfield, Jemma Goba, Brian Herdman, Matthew Holden-Jones, Tamlyn Jones, Gary Laitner, Peter Leadbetter, Tamara Littleton, Dave Maclean, Calum Nisbet, Sam Pennell, Stuart Price, Anne Pritchett, Mark Rogers, Mark Smith, Andy Street, Joanne Rule, Craig Tracy, Jonnie Turpie, Andrew Ward, Steve Ward, Justice Williams, Nick Venning, Rob Vickers, Lord Young, as well as every member of BNI Sunrise I had the pleasure of knowing. If I have missed you out, my sincere apologies; please know that I appreciate you.

Thanks to you, the reader, for getting this far. Please do get in touch. I would love to hear your story, your hopes and dreams.

A final thanks goes to my husband, Ben, for being the 15-year constant who made the *Ten Year Career* possible. Thanks for waking me up in the middle of the night with the idea for the framework! Thanks for humouring my ideas and always being there; the grittiest and best teammate I could have wished for.

Here's to the next chapter, whatever it may hold.

About The Author

Jodie is an entrepreneur, writer, powerlifter and avid traveller. She is the founder of JC Social Media, a company she began with a laptop and £800, and sold ten years later.

Throughout her business journey Jodie has been and continues to be a prolific writer. After winning Birmingham Young Professional of the Year at 25, the Great British Entrepreneur Awards Entrepreneurs Champion a few years later and securing a place on the Forbes 30 under 30 list of 2017, she joined Forbes as a regular contributor on the topic of entrepreneurs and gave a TEDx talk entitled 'Creating Useful People'.

Jodie has interviewed prominent figures for her Forbes articles, including personal development expert Robin Sharma, extreme athlete and world record holder Wim Hof, technology entrepreneur Jason Fried and spiritual author Gabrielle Bernstein.

Jodie's other books include *Stop Acting Like You're Going to Live Forever* volumes one and two, with accompanying guided journals; morning affirmation book *Daily Me*; and *Instagram Rules*, published with Quarto. She co-authored *How to Raise Entrepreneurial Kids* with entrepreneur Daniel Priestley and co-produced a series of children's books, *Clever Tykes*, which give entrepreneurial role models to six- to nine-year-olds and are read in every UK primary school.

Find Jodie online at jodiecook.com

Access the free *Ten Year Career* companion course at jodiecook.com/TYC